THE HEALTHY NEW MEXICAN KITCHEN

Copyright © 2024 by Chef's Palette

All rights reserved. No part of this book may be reproduced in any manner whatsoever without written permission except in the case of brief quotations embodied in critical articles and reviews.

First Printing, 2024

The Healthy New Mexican Kitchen

Embracing A Healthier Tradition

CHEF'S PALETTE

Cookbook

Contents

Disclaimer	1
Introduction	3
1 Salsas and Sauces	5

ROASTED HATCH GREEN CHILE SALSA

ROASTED CORN SALSA

CHILE PEQUIN SALSA

RED CHILE SAUCE

ROASTED HATCH GREEN CHILE SAUCE

2 Appetizers and Snacks	20

BAKED BLUE CORN NACHOS WITH GROUND TURKEY

SHRIMP COCKTAIL

HEALTHY NEW MEXICAN PIGS IN A BLANKET

HATCH GREEN CHILE MEATBALLS

3 Sides and Salads	33

QUELITES WITH CHILE PEQUIN

CALABACITAS

SMOKY PINTO BEANS

SPANISH RICE

ZESTY PASTA SALAD

4 Soups and Stews … 52

TURKEY POSOLE WITH DRIED RED CHILES

HATCH GREEN CHILE CHICKEN NOODLE SOUP

SOPA DE FIDEO

CARNE GUISADA CON PAPAS

ESTOFADO DE PESCADO (FISH STEW) USING TROUT

5 Breakfast … 70

EGG WHITE OMELET

HUEVOS RANCHEROS

CHORIZO AND EGG WHITE BURRITO

MACHACAS

BLUE CORN PANCAKES WITH FRESH FRUIT

6 Lunch … 83

HATCH GREEN CHILE TURKEY CHEESEBURGERS

BURRITO BOWLS

VEGGIE QUESADILLAS

BAKED CHICKEN TAQUITOS

GROUND TURKEY TOSTADAS WITH PINTO BEANS

7 Dinner   102

GRILLED FISH TACOS WITH CABBAGE SLAW

TURKEY ADOVADA

VEGETARIAN CHILE RELLENOS WITH QUINOA AND CHEESE

STEAK AND SHRIMP FAJITAS

VEGETARIAN TAMALES

8 Desserts   122

RICE PUDDING

ALMOND FLOUR BISCOCHITOS

GREEN CHILE APPLE PIE

RED CHILE BROWNIES

NATILLAS (NEW MEXICO CUSTARD)

9 Drinks   139

BLUE CORN ATOLE

SPICY CHAMPURRADO

HORCHATA

YERBA BUENA WITH LEMON

| 10 | Healthy Cooking Techniques and Tips | 153 |

CHOOSING THE RIGHT INGREDIENTS FOR HEALTHIER COOKING

TECHNIQUES TO ENHANCE FLAVOR WITHOUT EXTRA CALORIES

About Chef's Palette   159

Disclaimer

Food Allergies and Sensitivities
Important Notice to Readers

While the "Healthy New Mexican Kitchen" cookbook strives to provide diverse recipes catering to various dietary needs and food allergies, it is crucial for readers to take personal responsibility for their health and safety.

The following points serve as a disclaimer regarding food allergies and sensitivities:

- **Individual Responsibility:** Each individual is responsible for ensuring that the ingredients and cooking methods used are safe for their specific dietary needs and allergies. This includes being aware of any personal or family food allergies or sensitivities.
- **Ingredient Variations:** Ingredients can vary significantly in their allergen content due to brand differences, regional variations, and processing practices. Always read labels carefully and be aware of potential cross-contamination.
- **Professional Advice:** The information provided in this cookbook is not a substitute for professional medical advice, diagnosis, or treatment. Always seek the advice of your physician or other qualified health provider with any questions you may have regarding a medical condition or dietary restrictions.
- **Recipe Modifications:** While recipes in this cookbook offer suggestions for allergen-free alternatives, these substitutions may not be suitable for all individuals with food allergies or sensitivities. Personal discretion is advised.

- **Kitchen Safety:** When preparing meals for individuals with food allergies, it is essential to maintain a clean and safe kitchen environment to avoid cross-contamination.
- **Community Support:** If you're unsure about an ingredient or a recipe, consider reaching out to online communities or local support groups that specialize in dietary restrictions and food allergies for advice and shared experiences.
- **Continuous Learning:** Understanding and managing food allergies is an ongoing process. Stay informed about new findings, ingredients, and safe cooking practices.

- By acknowledging and understanding these points, readers can enjoy the "Healthy New Mexican Kitchen" cookbook while taking necessary precautions to ensure a safe and enjoyable cooking and dining experience, especially for those with specific dietary restrictions and food allergies.

Introduction

The History and Evolution of New Mexican Cuisine

New Mexican cuisine, a flavorful fusion of Native American and Spanish culinary traditions, has been evolving for centuries. This unique cuisine originated with the indigenous Pueblo people, who cultivated staples like corn, beans, and squash. The arrival of Spanish colonists in the 16th century introduced new ingredients like pork, dairy, and certain spices, which blended with the native foods and cooking methods to create the distinctive New Mexican fare we know today.

Chiles, both red and green, are the heart and soul of New Mexican dishes, providing not just heat but depth and complexity to every meal. Dishes like enchiladas, tamales, and chile rellenos have become synonymous with the region's cuisine. Over time, these dishes have evolved, but they always stay true to their roots, balancing the fiery chile with other local flavors.

Embracing Health in Traditional Flavors

In the "Healthy New Mexican Kitchen", we celebrate these traditional flavors while embracing a healthier perspective. This section of the book is dedicated to adapting classic New Mexican recipes to fit a more health-conscious lifestyle. Our goal is to create dishes that are lower in calories and carbohydrates but still rich in taste and cultural heritage.

We focus on incorporating ingredients with high nutrient density, using cooking techniques that preserve flavor while reducing fat and calorie content, and emphasizing lean proteins. Traditional dishes are reimagined, keeping the authentic essence but making them more accessible to those mindful of their dietary choices.

We steer clear of high-calorie, high-carb ingredients like white flour and certain high-starch vegetables. Instead, we embrace whole grains, lean meats, and an abundance of fresh vegetables. Herbs and spices play a crucial role, adding depth and complexity to dishes without the need for excess salt or fat.

This introduction serves as a guide to understanding the foundations of New Mexican cuisine and how it can be adapted to a healthier lifestyle. We delve into the history, the ingredients, and the culinary techniques that define this rich culinary heritage. Our recipes are more than just a list of ingredients; they are a celebration of culture, history, and the art of healthy living.

Chapter 1

Salsas and Sauces

Roasted Hatch Green Chile Salsa

- 6 servings

This Roasted Hatch Green Chile Salsa embodies the essence of New Mexican cuisine with a healthy twist. Made from freshly roasted Hatch green chiles, this salsa is not just a condiment but a celebration of New Mexico's most famous ingredient.

Ingredients:

- 4 medium-sized Hatch green chiles
- 2 medium tomatoes, diced
- 1 small onion, finely chopped
- 2 cloves garlic, minced
- 1/4 cup cilantro, finely chopped (optional, can be omitted)
- Juice of 1 lime
- 1/2 teaspoon cumin (ground)
- Salt to taste

Instructions:

1. **Roast the Chiles:** Preheat your oven to 400°F (200°C). Place the Hatch green chiles on a baking sheet and roast

them in the oven until the skins blister, about 15-20 minutes. Turn them occasionally to ensure even roasting.
2. **Peel and Chop Chiles:** Remove the chiles from the oven and let them cool. Once cool, peel off the skins, remove the seeds, and chop the chiles finely.
3. **Mix Ingredients:** In a mixing bowl, combine the roasted chiles, diced tomatoes, chopped onion, minced garlic, and cilantro (if using). Stir well.
4. **Season:** Add the lime juice, cumin, and salt to the salsa. Adjust the seasoning to your taste. Mix well.
5. **Refrigerate:** Allow the salsa to sit in the refrigerator for at least 30 minutes before serving. This resting period lets the flavors meld together.
6. **Serve:** Enjoy your Roasted Hatch Green Chile Salsa with your favorite dishes or as a healthy snack with baked tortilla chips.

Nutritional Information (per serving, based on 6 servings):

- **Calories:** 25
- **Carbohydrates:** 5g
- **Protein:** 1g
- **Fat:** 0g
- **Fiber:** 1g
- **Sodium:** 50mg

Chef's Note:

- This salsa is versatile and can be adjusted to your heat preference by using milder or hotter varieties of Hatch chiles. It's perfect for adding a flavorful kick to any meal while keeping it healthy and nutritious.

Roasted Corn Salsa

- 6 servings

Roasted corn salsa is a fresh and vibrant addition to any meal. This healthy New Mexican-inspired recipe captures the essence of traditional flavors while being mindful of nutrition.

Ingredients:

- 2 cups fresh corn kernels (about 2-3 ears of corn)
- 1 medium red onion, finely chopped
- 1 large ripe tomato, diced
- 1/2 cup fresh cilantro, chopped (optional, can be omitted)
- Juice of 1 lime
- 1 small jalapeño, seeded and finely chopped (adjust to taste)
- 1/4 teaspoon ground cumin
- Salt and pepper, to taste

Instructions:

1. **Prepare the Corn:** If using fresh corn, boil or grill the ears of corn until tender. Once cool, cut the kernels off the cob. If using frozen corn, thaw and drain it well.

2. **Combine Ingredients:** In a large bowl, mix together the corn kernels, red onion, tomato, and jalapeño. If you're including cilantro, add it as well.
3. **Season:** Sprinkle the mixture with ground cumin, salt, and pepper. Drizzle with lime juice and gently toss to combine.
4. **Chill:** For the flavors to meld, cover and refrigerate the salsa for at least 30 minutes before serving. This step is crucial for developing the full flavor profile.
5. **Serve:** Enjoy your corn salsa with baked tortilla chips, as a topping for grilled fish or chicken, or as a vibrant addition to salads and tacos.

Nutritional Information (per serving):

- **Calories:** 60
- **Carbohydrates:** 14g
- **Protein:** 2g
- **Fat:** 1g
- **Fiber:** 2g
- **Sodium:** Minimal (varies with added salt)

Chef's Note:

- Adjust the jalapeño quantity to suit your heat preference.
- For a smoky flavor, grill the corn instead of boiling it.
- This salsa is a perfect example of combining simple, fresh ingredients for a flavorful and healthy addition to your meals.

Chile Pequin Salsa

- 20 Servings (1 Tablespoon)

Chile Pequin, also known as bird pepper, is a small, fiery chile native to New Mexico. This salsa celebrates the intense heat and unique flavor of Chile Pequin in a healthy, low-calorie condiment that can liven up any dish.

Ingredients:

- 1/2 cup dried Chile Pequin peppers
- 2 medium tomatoes, diced
- 1 small onion, finely chopped
- 3 cloves garlic, minced
- 1/4 cup chopped fresh cilantro (optional, as you've mentioned avoiding cilantro)
- Juice of 1 lime
- 1 teaspoon apple cider vinegar
- 1/2 teaspoon ground cumin
- Salt to taste
- Water, as needed for consistency

Instructions:

1. **Preparation of Chile Pequin:** Start by wearing gloves to handle the Chile Pequin. These chilies are extremely hot,

and direct contact can irritate the skin. Gently rinse the peppers to remove any dust.
2. **Roasting:** In a dry skillet over medium heat, toast the Chile Pequin peppers for about 1-2 minutes, shaking the pan frequently. This process releases their natural oils and enhances the flavor. Be careful not to burn them.
3. **Blending:** Place the toasted Chile Pequin in a blender or food processor. Add diced tomatoes, chopped onion, minced garlic, lime juice, apple cider vinegar, ground cumin, and a little water. Blend until smooth. If the salsa is too thick, add a bit more water to reach your desired consistency.
4. **Seasoning:** Taste the salsa and adjust the salt as needed. Remember, the salsa will be quite spicy, so use salt to balance the flavors.
5. **Finishing Touches:** If you choose to use cilantro, stir it in at the end for a fresh, herbal flavor. However, this is optional based on your preference to avoid cilantro.
6. **Resting:** Allow the salsa to sit for at least an hour before serving. This resting period lets the flavors meld together beautifully.
7. **Serving:** Serve as a condiment with your favorite New Mexican dishes, tacos, or as a spicy dip for vegetables.

Nutritional Information (per serving):

- **Calories:** 5
- **Carbohydrates:** 1g
- **Protein:** 0g
- **Fat:** 0g
- **Sodium:** Minimal (varies with added salt)

Chef's Note:

- Chile Pequin is extremely spicy. Adjust the quantity to your heat preference.
- For a smokier flavor, you can char the tomatoes and garlic before blending.
- This salsa can be stored in the refrigerator for up to 1 week.

Red Chile Sauce

- About 2 cups

Red Chile Sauce, a cornerstone of New Mexican cuisine, is traditionally rich in flavor and robust in heat. In this healthier version, we use turkey broth for a lighter, leaner base, while still capturing the essence of this classic sauce.

Ingredients:

- 2 cups dried New Mexican red chiles, stemmed and seeded
- 3 cups turkey broth (low-sodium, fat-free)
- 1 medium onion, finely chopped
- 3 cloves garlic, minced
- 1 tsp ground cumin
- 1 tsp dried oregano (preferably Mexican)
- Salt, to taste
- 1 tbsp olive oil

Instructions:

1. **Prepare the Chiles:** Start by rehydrating the dried chiles. Place them in a bowl and cover with boiling water. Let them soak for about 30 minutes until they soften.

2. **Sauté Aromatics:** In a saucepan, heat the olive oil over medium heat. Add the chopped onions and sauté until translucent, about 5 minutes. Add the minced garlic and cook for another minute until fragrant.
3. **Blend Chiles:** Drain the chiles and transfer them to a blender. Add a cup of the turkey broth and blend until smooth. If the mixture is too thick, add a little more broth to help blend.
4. **Combine and Simmer:** Pour the chile mixture into the saucepan with the onions and garlic. Add the remaining turkey broth, cumin, oregano, and salt to taste.
5. **Cook the Sauce:** Bring the sauce to a boil, then reduce the heat and let it simmer for about 20-25 minutes. Stir occasionally. The sauce should thicken slightly and the flavors will meld together.
6. **Strain (Optional):** For a smoother sauce, strain it through a fine-mesh sieve to remove any solids.
7. **Adjust Seasoning:** Taste and adjust the seasoning, adding more salt if needed.
8. **Serve or Store:** Use the sauce immediately or let it cool and store in the refrigerator for up to a week. It can also be frozen for longer storage.

Nutritional Information (per serving):

- **Calories:** 50 kcal per 1/4 cup
- **Protein:** 2g
- **Carbohydrates:** 8g
- **Fat:** 2g
- **Sodium:** 150 mg (varies with salt usage)
- **Fiber:** 3g

Roasted Hatch Green Chile Sauce

- 4 cups of sauce

The Roasted Hatch Green Chile Sauce is a staple in New Mexican cuisine. This sauce celebrates the unique and vibrant flavor of Hatch green chiles, known for their perfect balance of heat and sweetness. This healthy version maintains the authentic taste while using ingredients that cater to a health-conscious diet.

Ingredients:

- 1 lb fresh Hatch green chiles
- 2 medium onions, finely chopped
- 4 cloves garlic, minced
- 2 tablespoons olive oil
- 2 cups vegetable broth (low sodium)
- 1 teaspoon ground cumin
- 1 teaspoon dried oregano
- Salt and pepper, to taste

Instructions:

1. **Roast the Chiles:** Preheat your oven to 400°F (200°C). Place the green chiles on a baking sheet and roast them in the oven for about 20-25 minutes, turning occasionally, until the skins are charred and blistered. Remove from the oven and let them cool. Once cooled, peel off the skins, remove the seeds, and chop the chiles finely.
2. **Sauté Onions and Garlic:** In a large saucepan, heat the olive oil over medium heat. Add the chopped onions and cook until they are translucent, about 5 minutes. Add the minced garlic and cook for an additional minute.
3. **Combine Ingredients:** Add the chopped green chiles to the saucepan along with the cumin, oregano, salt, and pepper. Stir well to combine.
4. **Add Broth and Simmer:** Pour in the vegetable broth and bring the mixture to a boil. Reduce the heat and let it simmer for about 20-30 minutes, or until the sauce thickens slightly..
5. **Serve and Enjoy:** Use the sauce immediately, or let it cool and store it in an airtight container in the refrigerator for up to a week.

Nutritional Information (per 1/4 cup serving):

- Calories: 30
- Carbohydrates: 4g
- Protein: 1g
- Fat: 1.5g
- Sodium: 50mg
- Fiber: 1g

Chef's Note:

- The heat level of Hatch green chiles can vary, so adjust the amount used according to your preference for spiciness.

Chapter 2

Appetizers and Snacks

Baked Blue Corn Nachos with Ground Turkey

- 4-6 Servings

This recipe offers a healthier twist on traditional nachos, featuring lean protein from ground turkey and the benefits of blue corn chips, which are higher in protein and fiber compared to regular tortilla chips. Enjoy this delicious, nutritious, and satisfying appetizer or snack!

Ingredients:

- 1 bag of blue corn tortilla chips
- 1 lb lean ground turkey
- 1 medium onion, finely chopped
- 2 cloves garlic, minced
- 1 tsp ground cumin
- 1 tsp chili powder
- 1/2 tsp smoked paprika (optional, for smoky flavor)
- Salt and pepper, to taste
- 1 cup low-fat shredded cheddar cheese
- 1/2 cup diced tomatoes
- 1/4 cup chopped green onions
- 1/4 cup sliced black olives

- 1/4 cup chopped fresh cilantro (optional, can be omitted)
- 1/2 cup low-fat sour cream or Greek yogurt (for serving)
- Salsa or pico de gallo (for serving)

Instructions:

1. **Preheat the Oven:** Preheat your oven to 375°F (190°C).
2. **Cook the Ground Turkey:** In a large skillet over medium heat, cook the ground turkey, breaking it apart with a spatula, until it's no longer pink. Drain any excess fat.
3. **Add Aromatics and Spices:** Add the chopped onion and minced garlic to the skillet with the turkey. Cook until the onions are translucent. Stir in cumin, chili powder, smoked paprika (if using), salt, and pepper. Cook for another 2 minutes, letting the flavors meld.
4. **Arrange the Chips:** Spread blue corn tortilla chips in a single layer on a large baking sheet.
5. **Assemble the Nachos:** Spoon the cooked turkey mixture over the chips. Sprinkle evenly with shredded cheese.
6. **Bake:** Place in the oven and bake for 8-10 minutes, or until the cheese is melted and bubbly.
7. **Add Toppings:** Remove from the oven and immediately top with diced tomatoes, green onions, black olives, and cilantro (if using).
8. **Serve:** Serve hot with sides of low-fat sour cream or Greek yogurt and salsa or pico de gallo.

Nutritional Information (per serving):

- **Calories:** 350 (approx.)
- **Protein:** 22g
- **Carbohydrates:** 30g
- **Fat:** 15g
- **Fiber:** 5g

- Sodium: 400mg

Shrimp Cocktail

- 4 Servings

This Shrimp Cocktail is a delightful mix of fresh and zesty flavors, perfect as a light appetizer. It's a healthy take on a classic dish, incorporating the vibrant tastes of New Mexican cuisine. Enjoy!

Ingredients:

- 16 large shrimp, peeled and deveined
- 1 cup tomato juice (low sodium preferred)
- 1/2 cup cucumber, finely diced
- 1/4 cup red onion, finely chopped
- 1/4 cup fresh lime juice
- 2 tablespoons fresh cilantro, chopped (optional, can be substituted with parsley)
- 1 jalapeño, seeded and finely chopped (adjust to taste)
- 1 avocado, diced
- 1 teaspoon Worcestershire sauce
- 1 teaspoon hot sauce (adjust to taste)
- Salt and pepper, to taste
- Lime wedges, for garnish

Instructions:

1. Cook the Shrimp:
   - Bring a pot of salted water to a boil.
   - Add the shrimp and cook until they are pink and opaque, about 2-3 minutes.
   - Remove the shrimp with a slotted spoon and place them in an ice bath to stop the cooking process.
   - Once cooled, drain and set aside.
2. Prepare the Cocktail Sauce:
   - In a medium bowl, combine the tomato juice, cucumber, red onion, lime juice, cilantro (or parsley), jalapeño, Worcestershire sauce, and hot sauce.
3. Season with salt and pepper to taste.
4. Mix well to combine all the ingredients.
5. Assemble the Shrimp Cocktail:
   - Spoon a generous amount of the sauce mixture into each glass.
   - Top with the cooked shrimp and diced avocado.
6. Garnish and Serve:
   - Garnish each glass with a lime wedge.
   - Serve chilled as a refreshing and healthy appetizer.

Nutritional Information (per serving):

- Calories: 150
- Protein: 12g
- Carbohydrates: 10g
- Fat: 7g
- Fiber: 3g
- Sodium: 150mg

Healthy New Mexican Pigs in a Blanket

Makes about 12-15 Pigs in a Blanket

"Pigs in a Blanket" is a beloved appetizer known for its simplicity and deliciousness. In our Healthy New Mexican Kitchen version, we give this classic a healthier twist, using whole-grain dough and lean meat to align with our health-conscious approach to New Mexican cuisine.

Ingredients

- 1 pound lean turkey sausage links
- 2 cups whole-grain flour
- 2 teaspoons baking powder
- 1/2 teaspoon salt
- 1/4 cup unsalted butter, chilled and cubed
- 3/4 cup skim milk
- 1 egg, beaten (for egg wash)
- Optional: 1/2 teaspoon smoked paprika for added flavor

Instructions:

1. **Preheat Oven:** Set your oven to 375°F (190°C) and line a baking sheet with parchment paper.
2. **Make the Dough:** In a large bowl, whisk together the whole-grain flour, baking powder, and salt. Add the chilled, cubed butter and use your fingers or a pastry blender to work the butter into the flour until it resembles coarse crumbs. Gradually add the milk, stirring until a soft dough forms.
3. **Roll and Cut the Dough:** On a lightly floured surface, roll out the dough to about 1/4 inch thickness. Cut the dough into strips that are wide enough to wrap around the sausages.
4. **Prepare Sausages:** If your sausages are not pre-cooked, lightly cook them in a skillet until just browned (they will continue cooking in the oven).
5. **Assemble:** Wrap each sausage in a strip of dough, sealing the edges. Place on the prepared baking sheet. If you like, brush each with a bit of beaten egg for a golden finish and sprinkle with smoked paprika.
6. **Bake:** Place in the oven and bake for 15-20 minutes, or until the dough is golden and puffed.
7. **Serve:** Let them cool slightly before serving. They can be enjoyed on their own or with a side of healthy, homemade salsa or a light dipping sauce.

Nutritional Information (per serving):

- Calories: Approximately 150-180
- Carbohydrates: 15g
- Protein: 10g
- Fat: 6g

Chef's Note:

- This recipe stays true to the flavors of New Mexican cuisine while being mindful of health. The whole-grain dough adds fiber and nutrients, while using lean turkey sausage cuts down on fat without sacrificing flavor. Enjoy these bite-sized delights guilt-free!

Hatch Green Chile Meatballs

- 4-6 servings

These Hatch Green Chile Meatballs combine the bold flavors of New Mexico with a focus on healthier ingredients, perfect for a nutritious and flavorful meal or snack. Enjoy the rich taste of Hatch green chiles in every bite!

Ingredients:

- 1 lb lean ground turkey
- 1/2 cup finely chopped Hatch green chiles (roasted, peeled, and seeded)
- 1/4 cup finely chopped onion
- 2 cloves garlic, minced
- 1/2 cup almond flour (as a binder)
- 1 large egg, beaten
- 1 tsp ground cumin
- 1 tsp dried oregano
- Salt and pepper, to taste
- 1 tbsp olive oil (for cooking)
- Fresh cilantro, chopped (for garnish; optional, as some may prefer to avoid cilantro)

Instructions:

1. **Preparation:** Preheat your oven to 375°F (190°C).
2. **Mix Ingredients:** In a large bowl, combine the ground turkey, Hatch green chiles, onion, garlic, almond flour, beaten egg, cumin, oregano, salt, and pepper. Mix well until all the ingredients are evenly distributed.
3. **Form Meatballs:** Scoop out small portions of the mixture and roll them into balls, approximately the size of a golf ball.
4. **Cook Meatballs:** Heat olive oil in a skillet over medium heat. Add the meatballs and cook until they are browned on all sides. This should take about 5-7 minutes.
5. **Bake:** Transfer the browned meatballs to a baking dish and place them in the preheated oven. Bake for 15-20 minutes, or until the meatballs are cooked through.
6. **Garnish and Serve:** Remove the meatballs from the oven and let them rest for a few minutes. If desired, garnish with chopped cilantro before serving.
7. **Serving Suggestion:** Serve the Hatch Green Chile Meatballs as an appetizer with toothpicks, or as a main course with a side of quinoa or a fresh salad.

Nutritional Information (per serving):

- **Calories:** 220
- **Protein:** 20g
- **Carbohydrates:** 4g
- **Fat:** 14g
- **Sugar:** 1g
- **Sodium:** Moderate
- **Fiber:** 1g

Chapter 3

Sides and Salads

Quelites with Chile Pequin

- 4 servings

Enjoy this heart-healthy, flavorful side dish that beautifully showcases the essence of New Mexican cuisine with a nutritious approach!

Ingredients:

- 2 bunches of fresh Quelites (wild spinach), thoroughly washed and chopped
- 1 tablespoon olive oil
- 2 cloves garlic, minced
- 1 small onion, finely chopped
- 1/2 cup vegetable broth (low sodium)
- 1 teaspoon chile pequin, crushed
- Salt, to taste
- Freshly ground black pepper, to taste
- 1/2 lemon, for juice

Instructions:

1. Preparation:

- Start by washing the quelites thoroughly under running water to remove any dirt or grit. Chop them roughly, including tender stems.

2. Sautéing Garlic and Onion:
    - In a large skillet, heat olive oil over medium heat. Add the minced garlic and chopped onion. Sauté until the onion becomes translucent and the garlic releases its aroma, about 3-4 minutes.

3. Cooking Quelites:
    - Add the chopped quelites to the skillet. Stir well to combine them with the garlic and onion. Sauté for about 2 minutes until the quelites start to wilt.

4. Adding Flavor:
    - Pour in the vegetable broth, and sprinkle the crushed chile pequin over the quelites. The chile pequin will add a delightful heat to the dish. Stir well to distribute the chile evenly.

5. Simmering:
    - Reduce the heat to low and let the quelites simmer in the broth for about 5-7 minutes. This allows the flavors to meld together and the quelites to become tender.

6. Seasoning:
    - Season with salt and freshly ground black pepper to taste. Be mindful of the amount of salt, as the chile pequin also adds to the overall saltiness.

7. Finishing Touch:
    - Before serving, squeeze fresh lemon juice over the cooked quelites. This adds a bright, citrusy note that complements the heat of the chile pequin.

8. Serving:
    - Serve the quelites warm as a side dish. They pair beautifully with grilled meats or can be enjoyed as a healthy, standalone vegetarian dish.

Nutritional Information (per serving):

- Calories: Approx. 60
- Carbohydrates: 6g
- Protein: 2g
- Fat: 3g
- Sodium: Low (varies with added salt)

Chef's Notes:

- Quelites are a traditional New Mexican green, known for their earthy flavor. They are highly nutritious, rich in vitamins and minerals.
- Chile pequin, a small but fiery chile, is a staple in New Mexican cooking, known for its intense heat and smoky flavor.
- This recipe is a healthy twist on traditional New Mexican cooking, highlighting local ingredients and flavors while keeping health in mind.

Calabacitas

- 4 servings

Calabacitas, a delightful New Mexican side dish, blends the sweetness of squash with the earthiness of green chiles. In this healthier version, we're focusing on the rich flavors of zucchini, yellow squash, and green chile, making it a perfect accompaniment to any main course.

Ingredients:

- 2 medium zucchinis, diced
- 2 medium yellow squashes, diced
- 1/2 cup onion, finely chopped
- 2 cloves garlic, minced
- 1 cup roasted green chiles, peeled, seeded, and chopped
- 2 tablespoons olive oil
- 1/2 teaspoon ground cumin
- Salt and pepper to taste
- 1/4 cup fresh cilantro, chopped (optional, avoid if you dislike cilantro)
- 1/2 cup grated low-fat cheese (cheddar or Monterey Jack)

Instructions:

1. Prepare the Ingredients:

- Wash and dice the zucchini and yellow squash.
- Finely chop the onion and mince the garlic.
- If using fresh green chiles, roast them over an open flame or in the oven, then peel, seed, and chop. Alternatively, use canned green chiles.

2. Cook the Vegetables:
   - In a large skillet, heat the olive oil over medium heat.
   - Add the onions and garlic, sautéing until the onions are translucent, about 3-4 minutes.
   - Add the diced zucchini and yellow squash to the skillet. Cook, stirring occasionally, until the vegetables are tender but still hold their shape, about 8-10 minutes.

3. Add Green Chiles and Seasonings:
   - Stir in the chopped green chiles and ground cumin.
   - Season with salt and pepper to taste.
   - Continue to cook for another 5 minutes, allowing the flavors to meld.

4. Final Touches:
   - Sprinkle the grated cheese over the top of the vegetables.
   - Cover the skillet and remove it from heat. Allow the residual heat to melt the cheese.

5. Serve and Enjoy:
   - Serve hot as a side dish with your favorite main course.

Nutritional Information (per serving):

- Calories: Approximately 150
- Protein: 6g
- Carbohydrates: 12g
- Fat: 9g (mostly unsaturated from olive oil)

- **Dietary Fiber:** 3g
- **Sugars:** 5g (natural sugars from vegetables)
- **Sodium:** Low (varies with added salt)

Smoky Pinto Beans

- 6-8 servings

This recipe for Smoky Pinto Beans incorporates the deep, rich flavors typical of New Mexican cuisine while being mindful of health and nutrition. Enjoy these beans as a hearty and flavorful addition to your meals!

Ingredients:

- 1 lb dried pinto beans, rinsed and sorted
- 6 cups water (for soaking)
- 4 cups low-sodium chicken or vegetable broth
- 1 large onion, finely chopped
- 2 cloves garlic, minced
- 1 teaspoon ground cumin
- 1/2 teaspoon oregano
- 1/2 teaspoon black pepper
- 1-2 tablespoons liquid smoke (adjust to taste)
- Salt, to taste
- Fresh cilantro, chopped (for garnish; optional)

Instructions:

1. **Pre-Soak Beans:** Place pinto beans in a large bowl and cover with about 6 cups of water. Let them soak

overnight, or at least 8 hours. After soaking, drain and rinse the beans.
2. **Cook the Beans:** In a large pot, combine the soaked beans with 4 cups of low-sodium broth. Bring to a boil, then reduce heat to maintain a gentle simmer. Cover and cook for 1 hour, stirring occasionally.
3. **Add Flavorings:** After the beans have simmered for an hour, add the chopped onion, minced garlic, cumin, oregano, black pepper, and liquid smoke. Stir well to combine.
4. **Continue Cooking:** Continue to simmer the beans, uncovered, for another 1 to 2 hours, or until the beans are tender and the liquid has thickened to your liking. Stir occasionally and add more broth or water if needed to keep beans just covered.
5. **Season:** Once the beans are tender, taste and adjust the seasoning with salt. Be cautious with salt if your broth is already salted.
6. **Serve:** Serve the smokey pinto beans hot, garnished with fresh cilantro if desired. They make a great side dish or can be used as a filling for burritos and tacos.

Nutritional Information (per serving):

- **Calories:** Approximately 150-200
- **Protein:** 10-12g
- **Carbohydrates:** 25-30g
- **Fiber:** 6-8g
- **Fat:** 1-2g
- **Sodium:** Varies based on broth and added salt

Chef's Note:

- **Liquid Smoke:** This is a potent flavoring made from condensing the smoke from burning wood. It imparts a deep, smoky flavor to dishes and is a great way to add the essence of smoked food without actual smoking.
- **Soaking Beans:** Soaking beans overnight helps in reducing cooking time and making them more digestible.
- **Herbs and Spices:** Feel free to adjust the herbs and spices according to your taste preferences.

Spanish Rice

· 4 servings

This Spanish Rice dish pairs wonderfully with grilled meats, fish, or can be enjoyed as a vegetarian meal on its own. It's a versatile side that brings the warmth and comfort of New Mexican cuisine to your table

Ingredients:

- 1 cup brown rice, uncooked
- 2 cups low-sodium chicken or vegetable broth
- 1 medium onion, finely chopped
- 2 cloves garlic, minced
- 1 large tomato, diced
- 1/2 cup diced red bell peppers (optional, can be substituted with another vegetable if avoiding bell peppers)
- 1/2 cup fresh or frozen corn kernels
- 1 teaspoon ground cumin
- 1/2 teaspoon chili powder
- 1/2 teaspoon smoked paprika (optional, can be omitted if avoiding paprika)
- 2 tablespoons olive oil
- Salt and pepper to taste
- Fresh cilantro, chopped (optional, can be omitted if avoiding cilantro)
- Lime wedges for serving

Instructions:

1. **Rinse the Rice:** Rinse brown rice under cold water until the water runs clear. This helps remove excess starch and improve texture.
2. **Sauté Aromatics:** In a large skillet, heat olive oil over medium heat. Add chopped onion and garlic, sautéing until the onion is translucent.
3. **Add Rice and Spices:** Stir in the brown rice, cumin, chili powder, and smoked paprika (if using). Cook for about 2 minutes, stirring frequently to coat the rice with the spices and lightly toast it.
4. **Add Liquids and Vegetables:** Add the diced tomato, bell peppers (or substitute), and corn to the skillet. Pour in the chicken or vegetable broth. Season with salt and pepper to taste.
5. **Simmer:** Bring the mixture to a boil, then reduce the heat to low. Cover and simmer for about 35-40 minutes, or until the rice is tender and the liquid is absorbed.
6. **Rest and Fluff:** Remove the skillet from heat and let it sit, covered, for 5 minutes. Then, fluff the rice with a fork.
7. **Garnish and Serve:** Garnish with chopped cilantro (if using) and serve with lime wedges.

Nutritional Information (per serving):

- **Calories:** 220
- **Protein:** 5g
- **Carbohydrates:** 45g
- **Fiber:** 4g
- **Fat:** 5g
- **Sodium:** Varies based on broth and added salt

Zesty Pasta Salad

- 6 servings

This pasta salad incorporates the bold flavors of New Mexican cuisine with healthy, nutrient-dense ingredients, making it a perfect side dish for any meal or a light lunch on its own. Enjoy this delicious blend of tradition and health!

Ingredients:

- 2 cups whole-grain pasta (like rotini or penne)
- 1 cup cherry tomatoes, halved
- 1/2 cup fresh corn kernels (or thawed if frozen)
- 1 medium zucchini, diced
- 1/2 cup chopped red onion
- 1/4 cup chopped fresh cilantro (optional, can be omitted if not preferred)
- 1/2 cup crumbled queso fresco or feta cheese
- 1/4 cup toasted pine nuts
- 1/4 cup diced roasted green chiles (Hatch chiles preferred)
- Salt and pepper, to taste

For the Dressing:

- 1/4 cup olive oil
- 2 tablespoons red wine vinegar
- 1 tablespoon lime juice

- 1 teaspoon honey or agave syrup
- 1/2 teaspoon ground cumin
- 1/2 teaspoon chili powder
- Salt and pepper, to taste

Instructions:

1. **Cook the Pasta:** In a large pot of boiling salted water, cook the pasta according to package instructions until al dente. Drain and rinse under cold water to stop the cooking process.
2. **Prepare the Vegetables:** In a large bowl, combine the halved cherry tomatoes, corn kernels, diced zucchini, chopped red onion, and diced green chiles.
3. **Make the Dressing:** In a small bowl, whisk together olive oil, red wine vinegar, lime juice, honey or agave syrup, ground cumin, and chili powder. Season with salt and pepper to taste.
4. **Combine:** Add the cooled pasta to the bowl with the vegetables. Pour the dressing over the pasta and vegetables and toss to combine.
5. **Add Cheese and Nuts:** Add the crumbled cheese and toasted pine nuts to the salad. Gently toss to mix.
6. **Season and Serve:** Adjust salt and pepper according to taste. Refrigerate for at least 30 minutes before serving to allow the flavors to meld together.
7. **Garnish:** Before serving, sprinkle with cilantro if using. Serve chilled or at room temperature.

Nutritional Information (per serving):

- Calories: 300
- Carbohydrates: 45g

- Protein: 10g
- Fat: 10g
- Fiber: 6g
- **Sodium:** Moderate (varies with cheese and added salt)

Chapter 4

Soups and Stews

Turkey Posole with Dried Red Chiles

- 6 servings

This Turkey Posole with Dried Red Chiles is a healthier twist on a classic New Mexican dish, rich in flavors and perfect for a comforting meal. The use of lean ground turkey and low-sodium broth makes it a heart-healthy option. Enjoy this wholesome and flavorful dish that embodies the essence of New Mexican cuisine!

Ingredients:

- 1 lb. lean ground turkey
- 6 cups low-sodium chicken broth
- 2 cups white hominy, drained and rinsed
- 1 medium onion, finely chopped
- 3 garlic cloves, minced
- 2 cups of water
- 6 dried red chile pods, stemmed and seeded
- 1 tsp. ground cumin
- 1 tsp. dried oregano (preferably Mexican)
- 1/2 tsp. black pepper
- Salt to taste
- Fresh cilantro, chopped (optional, for garnish)
- Lime wedges (for serving)

Instructions:

1. **Prepare the Chiles:** In a small pot, bring 2 cups of water to a boil. Remove from heat, add the dried red chiles, and let them soak for 20-30 minutes until they soften. Once softened, blend the chiles and their soaking water in a blender until smooth. Strain the mixture through a sieve to remove any solids and set aside.
2. **Cook the Turkey:** In a large pot, cook the ground turkey over medium heat until browned. Break up the meat with a spoon as it cooks.
3. **Sauté Vegetables:** Add the chopped onion and minced garlic to the pot with the turkey. Sauté until the onions are translucent, about 5 minutes.
4. **Combine Ingredients:** Add the chile sauce, chicken broth, hominy, cumin, oregano, black pepper, and salt to the pot. Stir well to combine all the ingredients.
5. **Simmer:** Bring the mixture to a boil, then reduce the heat to low and let it simmer, uncovered, for about 45 minutes to an hour. Stir occasionally. The posole should thicken slightly as it cooks.
6. **Adjust Seasonings:** Taste and adjust the seasonings as needed, adding more salt or pepper if necessary.
7. **Serve:** Ladle the posole into bowls. Garnish with fresh cilantro and serve with lime wedges on the side.

Nutritional Information (per serving):

- **Calories:** Approximately 250-300
- **Protein:** 20g
- **Carbohydrates:** 25g
- **Fat:** 8g
- **Fiber:** 5g
- **Sodium:** Low (varies with added salt)

Chef's Note:

- For a spicier posole, include some of the seeds from the dried chiles. For a milder version, make sure to remove all seeds.

Hatch Green Chile Chicken Noodle Soup

- 6 servings

This Hatch Green Chile Chicken Noodle Soup is a hearty and healthy take on a classic comfort dish, infused with the unique flavors of New Mexican cuisine.

Ingredients:

- 2 tablespoons olive oil
- 1 large onion, diced
- 3 cloves garlic, minced
- 1 1/2 cups diced carrots
- 1 cup diced celery
- 1 1/2 pounds boneless, skinless chicken breasts or thighs, cut into bite-sized pieces
- 4 cups low-sodium chicken broth
- 2 cups water
- 1 cup roasted, peeled, and chopped Hatch green chiles
- 1 teaspoon ground cumin
- 1 teaspoon dried oregano
- Salt and pepper, to taste
- 2 cups cooked whole wheat or high-fiber noodles

- 1/4 cup chopped fresh cilantro (optional, as some people prefer to avoid cilantro)
- Juice of 1 lime

Instructions:

1. **Heat the Olive Oil:** In a large pot, heat olive oil over medium heat. Add onions, garlic, carrots, and celery, cooking until the vegetables are softened, about 5 minutes.
2. **Cook the Chicken:** Add the chicken pieces to the pot. Cook until the chicken is no longer pink on the outside, about 5-7 minutes.
3. **Add Liquids and Chiles:** Pour in the chicken broth and water. Bring the mixture to a boil. Add the chopped Hatch green chiles, cumin, oregano, salt, and pepper. Reduce heat and let it simmer for about 20 minutes.
4. **Noodles:** If you haven't done so already, cook the noodles according to the package instructions. Once cooked, drain them and set aside.
5. **Combine and Finish Cooking:** Add the cooked noodles to the soup. Let everything simmer together for an additional 5 minutes so the flavors meld.
6. **Final Touches:** Remove the pot from heat. Stir in the fresh lime juice and chopped cilantro (if using).
7. **Serve:** Ladle the soup into bowls and serve hot. Optional: Garnish with additional cilantro or a lime wedge.

Nutritional Information (per serving):

- **Calories:** Approximately 250-300
- **Protein:** 25-30g
- **Carbohydrates:** 20-25g
- **Fiber:** 3-5g
- **Fat:** 8-10g

- **Sodium:** Low (varies with added salt)

Chef's Tip:

- **Roasting Chiles:** If you have fresh Hatch green chiles, roast them over an open flame or in the oven until the skin blisters. Peel, seed, and chop them for the soup.
- **Chicken Broth:** For a richer flavor, consider making your own low-sodium chicken broth.
- **Noodle Options:** Feel free to use any whole-grain or high-fiber noodle of your choice. For a gluten-free option, try rice noodles.

Sopa de Fideo

- 4 servings

Sopa de Fideo, a comforting Mexican noodle soup, is a staple in New Mexican cuisine. Our version stays true to its roots while offering a healthier twist, featuring whole-grain fideo noodles and an abundance of fresh vegetables.

Ingredients

- 1 tablespoon olive oil
- 1 small onion, finely chopped
- 2 cloves garlic, minced
- 1 medium carrot, diced
- 1 medium zucchini, diced
- 1 cup whole-grain fideo noodles or thin whole-wheat spaghetti, broken into short pieces
- 1 can (14.5 oz) diced tomatoes, with juice
- 4 cups low-sodium chicken or vegetable broth
- 1 teaspoon ground cumin
- 1 teaspoon dried oregano
- Salt and pepper, to taste
- Fresh cilantro (optional, for garnish)
- Lime wedges, for serving

Instructions

1. **Heat the Oil:** In a large pot, heat the olive oil over medium heat. Add the chopped onion and garlic, sautéing until the onion becomes translucent, about 3 minutes.
2. **Cook the Vegetables:** Add the diced carrot and zucchini to the pot. Cook for another 3-4 minutes, until the vegetables start to soften.
3. **Toast the Noodles:** Add the fideo noodles to the pot, stirring constantly. Toast the noodles until they turn a golden brown color, about 2 minutes.
4. **Add Tomatoes and Broth:** Pour in the diced tomatoes with their juice and the broth. Stir in the cumin and oregano. Season with salt and pepper to taste.
5. **Simmer the Soup:** Bring the mixture to a boil, then reduce the heat to low and let it simmer for 10-15 minutes, or until the noodles are cooked and the vegetables are tender.
6. **Serve:** Ladle the soup into bowls. Garnish with fresh cilantro if desired and serve with a wedge of lime on the side.

Nutritional Information (per serving)

- Calories: 180
- Carbs: 28g
- Protein: 6g
- Fat: 5g
- Sodium: 300mg
- Fiber: 4g

Chef's Tip:

- For a gluten-free version, use gluten-free pasta.
- Feel free to add other vegetables like bell peppers or celery for more variety.

- Chicken or turkey can be added for extra protein.

Carne Guisada con Papas

- 4-6 servings

This Carne Guisada with Potatoes recipe offers a hearty and flavorful meal that's in line with a healthier approach to traditional New Mexican cuisine. The use of lean beef, olive oil, and fresh vegetables ensures a nutritious and satisfying dish. Enjoy!

Ingredients:

- 2 lbs lean beef stew meat, cut into 1-inch cubes
- 2 tablespoons olive oil
- 1 large onion, diced
- 4 cloves garlic, minced
- 2 large tomatoes, diced
- 2 medium-sized potatoes, peeled and cubed
- 3 cups beef broth, low sodium
- 2 teaspoons ground cumin
- 1 teaspoon dried oregano
- 1 teaspoon smoked paprika
- Salt and pepper to taste
- Fresh cilantro for garnish (optional)
- 1 small jalapeño, finely chopped (optional for added heat)

Instructions:

1. **Prep the Meat:** Season the beef cubes with salt and pepper. In a large pot or Dutch oven, heat the olive oil over medium-high heat. Add the beef and brown on all sides, about 5-7 minutes. Remove the beef and set aside.
2. **Sauté the Vegetables:** In the same pot, add the diced onion and cook until translucent, about 3-4 minutes. Add the minced garlic and jalapeño (if using) and cook for an additional minute.
3. **Combine Ingredients:** Return the browned beef to the pot. Add the diced tomatoes, cubed potatoes, beef broth, cumin, oregano, and smoked paprika. Stir well to combine.
4. **Simmer:** Bring the mixture to a boil, then reduce the heat to low, cover, and let simmer for 1 to 1.5 hours, or until the beef is tender and the potatoes are cooked through.
5. **Adjust Seasonings:** Once the stew is cooked, taste and adjust the seasoning with salt and pepper as needed.
6. **Garnish and Serve:** Garnish with fresh cilantro before serving. Serve hot, paired with a side of whole-grain rice or a fresh salad for a complete meal.

Nutritional Information (per serving):

- **Calories:** 350
- **Protein:** 40g
- **Carbohydrates:** 20g
- **Fat:** 12g
- **Fiber:** 3g
- **Sodium:** 300mg

Estofado de Pescado (Fish Stew) Using Trout

- 4 servings

Estofado de Pescado is a traditional New Mexican fish stew known for its rich flavors and hearty ingredients. In this healthier version, we use trout, a lean and nutrient-rich fish, simmered in a savory tomato-based sauce with vegetables and spices, perfect for a nourishing and satisfying meal.

Ingredients:

- 4 trout fillets (about 6 ounces each), skin removed
- 2 tablespoons olive oil
- 1 large onion, chopped
- 3 cloves garlic, minced
- 1 bell pepper, diced (avoid for authenticity, optional for taste)
- 2 large tomatoes, diced
- 1 teaspoon ground cumin
- 1 teaspoon dried oregano
- 1/2 teaspoon ground coriander
- 1/4 teaspoon cayenne pepper (adjust to taste)
- Salt and pepper to taste

- 2 cups fish or vegetable broth
- 1 cup fresh or frozen corn kernels
- 1/4 cup chopped fresh cilantro (optional, avoid if not preferred)
- Lime wedges for serving

Instructions:

1. **Prepare the Trout:**
    - Pat the trout fillets dry with paper towels and season both sides with salt and pepper.
    - In a large pot, heat 1 tablespoon of olive oil over medium heat. Add the trout fillets and cook for 2-3 minutes on each side, or until they are just beginning to flake. Remove the trout from the pot and set aside.
2. **Cook the Vegetables:**
    - In the same pot, add the remaining olive oil. Sauté the onion and garlic until the onion is translucent, about 3-4 minutes.
    - Add the bell pepper (if using), tomatoes, cumin, oregano, coriander, cayenne pepper, salt, and pepper. Cook for another 5 minutes, stirring occasionally.
3. **Simmer the Stew:**
    - Pour in the broth and bring the mixture to a boil. Reduce the heat to low and let it simmer for about 10 minutes.
    - Gently add the trout fillets back into the pot. Add the corn and simmer for an additional 5 minutes, or until the fish is cooked through and the corn is tender.
4. **Final Touches:**
    - Taste and adjust the seasoning if necessary.

- If using cilantro, sprinkle it over the stew just before serving.

5. **Serve:**
   - Carefully ladle the stew into bowls, ensuring each serving gets a piece of trout.
   - Serve with lime wedges on the side for a fresh burst of flavor.

Nutritional Information (per serving):

- Calories: Approximately 250-300
- Protein: 25-30g
- Carbohydrates: 15-20g
- Fat: 10-15g
- Sodium: 300mg
- Fiber: 2-3g

Chef's Note:

- Nutritional values are approximate and may vary depending on the specific ingredients used.

Serving Suggestion:

- Pair this hearty stew with a side of quinoa or a slice of whole-grain tortilla for a complete meal.

Chapter 5

Breakfast

Egg White Omelet

- 1 serving

Savor the flavors of New Mexico with this light and nutritious egg white omelet. Packed with fresh vegetables and herbs, this dish is a perfect start to your day, embodying the essence of New Mexican cuisine in a health-conscious way.

Ingredients:

- 3 large egg whites
- 1/4 cup diced green chiles (Hatch chiles if available)
- 1/4 cup chopped tomatoes
- 2 tablespoons finely chopped onions
- 1/4 cup chopped fresh spinach
- 1/4 cup shredded low-fat cheese (optional)
- 1 teaspoon olive oil
- Salt and pepper to taste
- Fresh cilantro for garnish (optional)

Instructions:

1. Prepare the Vegetables:
    - Wash and finely chop the tomatoes, onions, and spinach. If using fresh green chiles, roast them over an open flame or in the oven, peel, deseed, and chop.

2. **Whisk the Egg Whites:**
   - In a bowl, whisk the egg whites with a pinch of salt and pepper until frothy.
3. **Cook the Omelet:**
   - Heat olive oil in a non-stick skillet over medium heat.
   - Sauté onions and tomatoes for about 2 minutes until the onions are translucent.
   - Add the green chiles and spinach to the skillet and cook for an additional minute.
   - Pour the egg whites over the vegetables, tilting the pan to spread them evenly.
   - As the egg begins to set, lift the edges gently with a spatula and tilt the pan to allow uncooked egg to flow underneath.
   - When the eggs are set but still slightly moist, sprinkle shredded cheese on one half of the omelet (if using).
4. **Fold and Serve:**
   - Carefully fold the omelet in half with the spatula and slide it onto a plate.
   - Garnish with fresh cilantro if desired.

Nutritional Information (per serving, without cheese):

- **Calories:** 120
- **Protein:** 14g
- **Carbohydrates:** 4g
- **Fat:** 5g
- **Sodium:** 170mg
- **Fiber:** 1g

Huevos Rancheros

- 4 Servings

Huevos Rancheros, a classic New Mexican breakfast, is a hearty and flavorful dish. In our healthy version, we focus on using fresh, low-calorie ingredients while maintaining the authentic flavors of this beloved dish.

Ingredients:

- 4 whole grain tortillas
- 8 eggs
- 1 cup of homemade red chile sauce (use turkey broth for a healthier version)
- 1 cup black beans, cooked and drained (substitute for pinto beans if preferred)
- 2 medium tomatoes, diced
- 1 small onion, finely chopped
- 2 cloves garlic, minced
- 1 teaspoon olive oil
- 1/2 cup low-fat cheese, shredded (optional)
- Salt and pepper, to taste
- Fresh cilantro for garnish (optional, as some may avoid cilantro)
- 1 avocado, sliced (for serving)

Instructions:

1. **Prepare the Toppings:** In a skillet, heat olive oil over medium heat. Add onions and garlic, sautéing until softened. Add tomatoes and cook for another 2-3 minutes. Stir in the cooked beans, season with salt and pepper, and keep warm.
2. **Cook the Eggs:** In another non-stick skillet, cook the eggs to your preference (over-easy, over-medium, or scrambled). Season with salt and pepper.
3. **Warm the Tortillas:** Heat the tortillas in a dry skillet or in the oven until warm and slightly crispy.
4. **Assemble the Dish:** Place a warm tortilla on each plate. Top each tortilla with two cooked eggs, a generous spoonful of the bean and tomato mixture, and a drizzle of the red chile sauce.
5. **Add Toppings:** Sprinkle with shredded low-fat cheese, if using. Garnish with sliced avocado and optional cilantro.
6. **Serve:** Serve immediately while warm.

Nutritional Information (per serving):

- **Calories:** 350
- **Carbs:** 40g
- **Protein:** 20g
- **Fat:** 15g
- **Fiber:** 8g
- **Sodium:** Low (varies with added salt)

Chorizo and Egg White Burrito

- 4 servings

This recipe for Chorizo Egg White Wraps is a healthy twist on a traditional New Mexican breakfast. It combines lean protein from turkey chorizo and egg whites with the wholesome goodness of vegetables, all wrapped in a whole grain tortilla. Perfect for a nutritious and satisfying start to your day!

Ingredients:

- **Egg Whites:** 8 (from large eggs)
- **Lean Turkey Chorizo:** 1 cup, crumbled
- **Spinach:** 1 cup, fresh
- **Whole Grain Tortillas:** 4 medium-sized
- **Low-fat Cheese:** ½ cup, shredded (optional)
- **Onion:** ¼ cup, finely chopped
- **Tomato:** 1 medium, diced
- **Garlic:** 1 clove, minced
- **Olive Oil:** 1 tablespoon
- **Salt:** To taste
- **Pepper:** To taste

Instructions:

1. **Prepare the Chorizo:**
   - Heat a non-stick skillet over medium heat.
   - Add the crumbled turkey chorizo and cook until it's browned and cooked through, about 5-7 minutes. Set aside.
2. **Cook the Vegetables:**
   - In the same skillet, add olive oil, chopped onions, and minced garlic.
   - Sauté for 2-3 minutes until the onions are translucent.
   - Add the diced tomato and cook for another 2 minutes.
   - Stir in the fresh spinach and cook until just wilted. Remove from heat.
3. **Make the Egg Whites:**
   - In a separate non-stick skillet, lightly coated with cooking spray, pour in the egg whites.
   - Cook over medium heat, stirring occasionally, until the egg whites are fully cooked.
   - Season with salt and pepper to taste.
4. **Assemble the Wraps:**
   - Warm the whole grain tortillas on a skillet for about 30 seconds on each side.
   - Lay out the tortillas and distribute the cooked egg whites evenly among them.
   - Add the cooked chorizo and the vegetable mixture over the egg whites.
   - Sprinkle with low-fat cheese if using.
5. **Roll the Wraps:**
   - Fold in the sides of each tortilla and roll them up tightly.

Nutritional Information (per serving):

- **Calories:** Approximately 250-300 kcal
- **Protein:** 20g
- **Carbohydrates:** 20g
- **Fats:** 10g
- **Fiber:** 3g
- **Sodium:** Low (varies with added salt)

Machacas

- 4 servings

This healthier version of Machacas maintains the authentic flavors of New Mexican cuisine while keeping an eye on nutritional balance, making it a perfect addition to your healthy diet.

Ingredients:

- 1 lb lean beef flank steak
- 4 large eggs
- 2 medium tomatoes, diced
- 1 medium onion, finely chopped
- 2 cloves garlic, minced
- 1/2 cup green chiles, chopped (Hatch chiles preferred for authenticity)
- 1 tsp cumin powder
- 1/2 tsp chili powder
- Salt and pepper, to taste
- 1 tbsp olive oil
- Whole wheat tortillas, for serving
- Fresh salsa, for serving

Instructions:

1. Preparation of Beef:

- Cook the beef flank steak in a slow cooker with enough water to cover it for about 6-8 hours on low heat until it is tender and can be easily shredded.
- Once cooked, remove the beef, let it cool, and then shred it into thin strips.

2. **Sautéing Vegetables:**
   - In a large skillet, heat olive oil over medium heat.
   - Add the chopped onions and garlic, sautéing until the onions become translucent.
   - Add the diced tomatoes, green chiles, cumin, chili powder, salt, and pepper. Cook for about 5 minutes until the tomatoes soften.

3. **Combining Beef and Eggs:**
   - Add the shredded beef to the skillet and mix well with the vegetables.
   - Whisk the eggs in a bowl and pour them over the beef mixture in the skillet.
   - Stir gently and cook until the eggs are set, about 3-4 minutes.

4. **Serving:**
   - Serve the Machacas with warm whole wheat tortillas.
   - Garnish with fresh salsa on the side.

Nutritional Information (per serving):

- **Calories:** Approx. 300
- **Carbs:** 15g
- **Protein:** 35g
- **Fat:** 12g
- **Fiber:** 3g
- **Sugar:** 2g
- **Sodium:** Low (varies on salt added)

Blue Corn Pancakes with Fresh Fruit

- Makes about 8 pancakes, serving size 2 pancakes.

Enjoy these healthy and delicious Blue Corn Pancakes with Fresh Fruit, a perfect start to your day, combining traditional New Mexican ingredients with a focus on health and flavor!

Ingredients:

- 1 cup blue cornmeal
- 3/4 cup whole wheat flour
- 1 tablespoon baking powder
- 1/4 teaspoon salt
- 1 tablespoon honey or agave syrup
- 1 egg, lightly beaten
- 1 cup almond milk or skim milk
- 2 tablespoons canola oil or melted coconut oil
- 1/2 teaspoon vanilla extract
- Cooking spray for the griddle
- Fresh fruit for topping (berries, sliced banana, or apple)

Instructions:

1. **Mix Dry Ingredients:** In a large bowl, whisk together blue cornmeal, whole wheat flour, baking powder, and salt.
2. **Combine Wet Ingredients:** In a separate bowl, whisk together honey, beaten egg, almond milk, oil, and vanilla extract.
3. **Combine Wet and Dry:** Pour the wet ingredients into the dry ingredients. Stir until just combined. Be careful not to overmix; the batter should be a bit lumpy.
4. **Preheat Griddle:** Heat a griddle or non-stick pan over medium heat. Coat with cooking spray to prevent sticking.
5. **Cook Pancakes:** Pour 1/4 cup of batter for each pancake onto the griddle. Cook until bubbles form on the surface, then flip and cook until browned on the other side.
6. **Serve with Fresh Fruit:** Serve the pancakes hot, topped with a generous helping of fresh fruit.

Nutritional Information (per serving):

- **Calories:** 200 (varies with choice of fruit and syrup)
- **Protein:** 6g
- **Carbohydrates:** 35g
- **Fat:** 5g
- **Fiber:** 4g
- **Sugar:** 6g (natural sugars from fruit)
- **Sodium:** Moderate

Chapter 6

Lunch

Hatch Green Chile Turkey Cheeseburgers

- 4 servings

This Hatch Green Chile Turkey Cheeseburger offers a healthier twist on a classic, incorporating the bold flavors of New Mexican cuisine with a lean, nutritious approach. Enjoy this delightful blend of spicy, savory, and fresh ingredients in a wholesome burger that satisfies your cravings and supports your health goals!

Ingredients:

- 1 pound ground turkey (preferably lean)
- 1/2 cup finely chopped roasted Hatch green chiles
- 1 teaspoon ground cumin
- 1/2 teaspoon garlic powder
- 1/2 teaspoon onion powder
- Salt and pepper, to taste
- 4 whole-grain hamburger buns
- 4 slices of low-fat cheddar cheese
- Lettuce leaves
- Thinly sliced tomato
- Thinly sliced red onion

- Low-fat mayonnaise or Greek yogurt (optional)
- Fresh cilantro leaves (avoid if you dislike cilantro)

Instructions:

1. **Preparation of Turkey Patties:**
    - In a large bowl, combine the ground turkey, chopped Hatch green chiles, cumin, garlic powder, and onion powder. Season with salt and pepper to taste.
    - Mix the ingredients gently until well combined. Be careful not to overmix, as this can make the patties tough.
    - Divide the mixture into 4 equal portions and form each into a patty.
2. **Cooking the Patties:**
    - Preheat a grill or skillet over medium heat.
    - Place the turkey patties on the grill or skillet. Cook for about 5-7 minutes per side or until fully cooked. The internal temperature should reach 165°F (74°C).
    - A couple of minutes before the patties are done, place a slice of cheese on each patty to melt.
3. **Assembling the Burgers:**
    - Toast the whole-grain buns lightly on the grill or in a toaster.
    - Spread a thin layer of low-fat mayonnaise or Greek yogurt on the buns, if desired.
    - On each bun bottom, place a lettuce leaf, followed by the cooked turkey patty with cheese.
    - Add slices of tomato and red onion on top of the cheese.
    - If using, sprinkle some fresh cilantro leaves over the toppings.
    - Cover with the top half of the bun.
4. **Serving:**

- Serve the burgers hot with a side of baked sweet potato fries or a fresh garden salad for a balanced meal.

Nutritional Information (per serving):

- **Calories:** 350-400 (approx.)
- **Protein:** 30g
- **Carbohydrates:** 35g
- **Fat:** 15g (varies with the leanness of the meat and choice of cheese)
- **Fiber:** 6g
- **Sodium:** Moderate

Burrito Bowls

- 4 servings

This Burrito Bowl recipe captures the essence of New Mexican flavors in a nutritious and delicious way, perfect for a health-conscious approach to traditional dishes!

Ingredients:

- 2 cups cauliflower rice (as a low-carb alternative to traditional rice)
- 1 lb lean chicken breast, grilled and sliced
- 1 cup black beans (rinsed and drained)
- 1 cup corn kernels (fresh or frozen)
- 1 large avocado, sliced
- 1 cup cherry tomatoes, halved
- 1/2 cup red onion, finely chopped
- 1 cup romaine lettuce, shredded
- 1/2 cup low-fat shredded cheese (optional)
- 1/4 cup Greek yogurt (as a sour cream substitute)
- 1 lime, cut into wedges
- 2 tbsp cilantro, chopped (optional, as some people may prefer to avoid it)
- Salt and pepper, to taste
- 1 tsp ground cumin
- 1 tsp chili powder
- Olive oil spray

Instructions:

1. **Prepare the Cauliflower Rice:**
    - Rinse the cauliflower and pat dry. Grate the cauliflower using a box grater or food processor until it resembles rice grains.
    - Heat a non-stick skillet over medium heat. Spray lightly with olive oil spray. Add the grated cauliflower, season with salt and pepper, and sauté for 5-7 minutes until tender. Set aside.
2. **Season and Grill the Chicken:**
    - Season the chicken breasts with salt, pepper, cumin, and chili powder.
    - Grill the chicken over medium-high heat for 5-6 minutes on each side, or until fully cooked. Let it rest for a few minutes, then slice into strips.
3. **Assemble the Bowls:**
    - Divide the cauliflower rice among four bowls.
    - Top each bowl with equal portions of grilled chicken, black beans, corn, avocado slices, cherry tomatoes, and red onion.
    - Add a sprinkle of shredded cheese and a dollop of Greek yogurt on top of each bowl.
    - Garnish with lime wedges and chopped cilantro, if desired.
4. **Serve:**
    - Serve the burrito bowls immediately, allowing each person to squeeze lime juice over their bowl to taste. Enjoy a flavorful and healthy New Mexican-style lunch!

Nutritional Information (per serving):

- **Calories:** Approximately 350
- **Protein:** 28g
- **Carbohydrates:** 25g (Net carbs: 18g)
- **Fat:** 15g
- **Fiber:** 7g
- **Sodium:** Moderate

Veggie Quesadillas

- 4 servings

This Veggie Quesadilla is a delicious and nutritious twist on a New Mexican classic, perfect for a healthy lunch or dinner. Enjoy the blend of flavors and textures in this easy-to-make, heart-healthy dish.

Ingredients:

- 4 whole-grain tortillas
- 1 cup low-fat shredded cheese (preferably a blend of cheddar and Monterey Jack)
- 1 medium zucchini, thinly sliced
- 1 red bell pepper, thinly sliced (optional, can be replaced with another vegetable if preferred)
- 1 cup spinach, roughly chopped
- 1/2 cup corn kernels (fresh or frozen)
- 1/2 cup canned black beans, rinsed and drained
- 1/2 red onion, thinly sliced
- 1 teaspoon olive oil
- 1 teaspoon ground cumin
- 1/2 teaspoon garlic powder
- Salt and pepper, to taste
- Fresh cilantro for garnish (optional)
- Salsa and Greek yogurt for serving (instead of sour cream)

Instructions:

1. **Prep the Vegetables:** Heat olive oil in a large skillet over medium heat. Add the zucchini, red bell pepper, and red onion. Sauté for 4-5 minutes until they start to soften. Add the corn, black beans, cumin, garlic powder, salt, and pepper. Cook for another 2-3 minutes. Set aside.
2. **Assemble the Quesadillas:** Lay out the whole-grain tortillas on a flat surface. Sprinkle half of each tortilla with the shredded cheese. Top the cheese with a generous amount of the sautéed vegetable mixture and then some spinach. Fold the tortillas in half over the filling.
3. **Cook the Quesadillas:** Heat a non-stick skillet or griddle over medium heat. Place the folded quesadillas on the skillet and cook for about 2-3 minutes on each side, or until the tortillas are golden brown and the cheese has melted.
4. **Serve:** Cut each quesadilla into wedges. Serve hot with salsa and a dollop of Greek yogurt, and garnish with fresh cilantro if desired.

Nutritional Information (per serving):

- **Calories:** 280
- **Carbohydrates:** 34g
- **Protein:** 15g
- **Fat:** 10g
- **Fiber:** 6g
- **Sodium:** 480mg

Baked Chicken Taquitos

- Makes 8-10 taquitos, ideal for 4 servings (2-3 taquitos per serving)

Baked Taquitos are a healthier version of the traditional fried taquitos. This dish combines the authentic flavors of New Mexican cuisine with a health-conscious approach, ensuring a delightful experience that's both tasty and nutritious.

Ingredients

- 2 cups cooked, shredded chicken breast (can substitute with turkey or a vegetarian protein like tofu)
- 1 cup cooked black beans (rinsed and drained if using canned)
- 1/2 cup corn kernels (fresh or frozen)
- 1/2 cup diced tomatoes (fresh or canned without added sugar)
- 1/2 cup diced onion
- 2 cloves garlic, minced
- 1/2 cup low-fat cheese (cheddar or Monterey Jack), shredded
- 1 tsp ground cumin
- 1 tsp chili powder
- Salt and pepper to taste

- 8-10 whole wheat or corn tortillas
- Cooking spray

Instructions

1. **Preheat Oven:** Preheat your oven to 400°F (200°C). Line a baking sheet with parchment paper or lightly grease it.
2. **Prepare Filling:** In a large bowl, combine the shredded chicken, black beans, corn, tomatoes, onion, garlic, cheese, cumin, and chili powder. Season with salt and pepper to taste. Mix well.
3. **Soften Tortillas:** To make the tortillas more pliable, wrap them in a damp cloth and microwave for about 20-30 seconds.
4. **Assemble Taquitos:** Place a tortilla on a flat surface. Spoon about 2-3 tablespoons of the filling onto the lower third of the tortilla. Roll the tortilla tightly around the filling.
5. **Arrange on Baking Sheet:** Place the rolled taquito seam-side down on the prepared baking sheet. Repeat with the remaining tortillas and filling.
6. **Spray and Bake:** Lightly spray the tops of the taquitos with cooking spray. This will help them turn golden brown and crisp in the oven. Bake for 20-25 minutes, or until the taquitos are crispy and lightly browned.
7. **Serve:** Let them cool for a few minutes before serving. Enjoy your baked taquitos with salsa, guacamole, or a light sour cream dip.

Nutritional Information (per taquito):

- Calories: ~150-200 kcal
- Protein: 10-15 g
- Carbohydrates: 20-25 g

- Fat: 4-6 g
- Fiber: 3-4 g
- Sodium: Moderate

Ground Turkey Tostadas with Pinto Beans

- 4 servings

This Ground Turkey Tostada is a healthy and delicious take on a traditional New Mexican dish. It's rich in protein and fiber, making it a satisfying and nutritious meal. Enjoy the blend of flavors and the freshness of each ingredient in every bite!

Ingredients:

- For the Ground Turkey:
- 1 lb lean ground turkey
- 1 medium onion, finely chopped
- 2 cloves garlic, minced
- 1 tsp ground cumin
- 1/2 tsp chili powder
- 1/2 tsp dried oregano
- Salt and pepper, to taste
- For the Tostadas:
- 4 whole-grain tostada shells
- 2 cups cooked pinto beans, mashed
- 1 cup shredded lettuce
- 1 medium tomato, diced

- 1/2 cup reduced-fat shredded cheese (optional)
- 1/4 cup plain Greek yogurt
- Fresh cilantro, chopped (optional, for garnish)
- Lime wedges, for serving

Instructions:

1. **Cook the Ground Turkey:**
   - Heat a non-stick skillet over medium heat. Add the ground turkey and cook, breaking it apart with a spoon, until browned.
   - Add the onion, garlic, cumin, chili powder, oregano, salt, and pepper. Cook for another 5-7 minutes, stirring occasionally, until the onion is soft and the spices are fragrant.
2. **Prepare the Tostadas:**
   - Preheat your oven to 375°F (190°C).
   - Place tostada shells on a baking sheet and warm in the oven for 3-5 minutes.
3. **Assemble the Tostadas:**
   - Spread a layer of mashed pinto beans on each tostada shell.
   - Top with the cooked ground turkey.
   - Add shredded lettuce and diced tomato.
   - Sprinkle with shredded cheese, if using.
   - Dollop a spoonful of Greek yogurt on top.
4. **Garnish and Serve:**
   - Garnish with fresh cilantro, if desired.
   - Serve with lime wedges on the side.

Nutritional Information (per serving):

- Calories: 350 kcal

- Protein: 28 g
- Fat: 12 g
- Carbohydrates: 35 g
- Fiber: 8 g
- Sugar: 3 g

Chapter 7

Dinner

Grilled Fish Tacos with Cabbage Slaw

- 4 servings (2 tacos per serving)

This recipe for Grilled Fish Tacos with Cabbage Slaw is a healthy, flavorful, and satisfying dish that perfectly embodies the spirit of New Mexican cuisine with a health-conscious twist. Enjoy this delicious and nutritious meal!

Ingredients:

For the Fish Tacos:

- 4 medium-sized trout filets (about 6 oz each)
- 2 tbsp olive oil
- 1 tsp ground cumin
- 1 tsp garlic powder
- 1 tsp chili powder
- Salt and pepper, to taste
- 8 whole-grain tortillas

For the Cabbage Slaw:

- 2 cups shredded red cabbage
- 1 cup shredded carrot
- 1/4 cup finely chopped red onion

- 1/4 cup chopped fresh cilantro (if using)
- 2 tbsp apple cider vinegar
- 1 tbsp extra-virgin olive oil
- Juice of 1 lime
- Salt and pepper, to taste

Optional Toppings:

- Diced avocado
- Fresh salsa
- Lime wedges

Instructions

1. **Prepare the Cabbage Slaw:**
    - In a large bowl, combine the shredded cabbage, carrot, red onion, and cilantro (if using).
    - In a small bowl, whisk together the apple cider vinegar, olive oil, and lime juice. Pour over the cabbage mixture and toss to coat evenly. Season with salt and pepper. Set aside to marinate.
2. **Season the Fish:**
    - Preheat your grill to medium-high heat.
    - Pat the trout fillets dry with paper towels. Brush each side with olive oil.
    - In a small bowl, mix together the cumin, garlic powder, chili powder, salt, and pepper. Sprinkle the spice mix evenly over both sides of the fillets.
3. **Grill the Fish:**
    - Place the trout fillets on the grill and cook for about 3-4 minutes on each side, or until the fish flakes easily with a fork.

- Remove the fish from the grill and let it rest for a few minutes. Then, break the fillets into smaller pieces suitable for tacos.

4. **Warm the Tortillas:**
   - Place tortillas on the grill for about 30 seconds on each side, just until they are warm and slightly charred.

5. **Assemble the Tacos:**
   - Place a portion of the grilled fish onto each tortilla.
   - Top with a generous helping of the cabbage slaw.
   - Add any optional toppings like diced avocado or fresh salsa.
   - Serve with lime wedges on the side.

Nutritional Information (per serving)

- **Servings:** 4 (2 tacos per serving)
- **Calories:** Approximately 350-400 kcal
- **Protein:** 24g
- **Carbohydrates:** 35g
- **Fat:** 16g (Varies with toppings)

Chef's Note:

- For extra flavor, marinate the fish in a mixture of lime juice, olive oil, and spices for about 30 minutes before grilling.
- Ensure the grill is hot enough to prevent the fish from sticking.
- Feel free to customize the toppings based on your preferences and dietary needs.

Turkey Adovada

- 4-6 servings

Turkey Carne Adovada is a healthier twist on a classic New Mexican dish. Traditionally made with pork, this recipe uses lean turkey, marinated in a blend of red chiles and spices, then slow-cooked to perfection. It's a flavorful, comforting dish that brings warmth and rich taste to your table.

Ingredients:

- 2 lbs lean turkey breast, cut into cubes
- 4 New Mexico red chiles, dried
- 2 cups chicken or turkey broth, low sodium
- 1 medium onion, finely chopped
- 3 garlic cloves, minced
- 1 tsp cumin
- 1 tsp oregano, dried
- ½ tsp cinnamon
- Salt and pepper, to taste
- 2 tbsp apple cider vinegar
- Olive oil, for cooking

Instructions:

1. Chile Paste Preparation:

- Remove stems and seeds from the dried chiles. Soak them in hot water for about 20 minutes until they soften.
- Drain the chiles and place them in a blender. Add 1 cup of broth, garlic, cumin, oregano, cinnamon, apple cider vinegar, salt, and pepper. Blend until smooth.

2. **Marinate the Turkey:**
   - In a large bowl, coat the turkey pieces with the chile paste. Cover and refrigerate for at least 4 hours, preferably overnight, to marinate.

3. **Cooking:**
   - Heat a little olive oil in a large pot over medium heat. Sauté the onions until translucent.
   - Add the marinated turkey and cook until it's browned on all sides.
   - Pour in the remaining broth and bring to a boil.
   - Reduce the heat to low, cover, and simmer for about 1-1.5 hours, or until the turkey is tender.

4. **Finishing Touches:**
   - If the sauce is too thin, you can simmer it uncovered for a few more minutes to thicken.
   - Taste and adjust the seasoning if necessary.

5. **Serving:**
   - Serve hot with a side of cauliflower rice, or wrapped in lettuce leaves for a low-carb option.

Nutritional Information (per serving):

- Calories: Approx. 300-350
- Carbohydrates: <10g
- Protein: 35-40g
- Fat: 10-15g

- Sodium: Moderate

Vegetarian Chile Rellenos with Quinoa and Cheese

- 4 servings

Enjoy this healthy and flavorful take on a traditional New Mexican dish!

Ingredients:

- 4 large New Mexico green chiles, roasted and peeled
- 1 cup cooked quinoa
- 1/2 cup corn kernels (fresh or frozen)
- 1/2 cup black beans, rinsed and drained
- 1/2 cup diced tomatoes (fresh or canned)
- 1/4 cup red onion, finely chopped
- 1 garlic clove, minced
- 1/2 cup low-fat cheese (cheddar or Monterey Jack), shredded
- 1 teaspoon cumin
- 1/2 teaspoon smoked paprika (optional, for smoky flavor)
- Salt and pepper to taste
- 2 eggs, beaten
- 1/2 cup whole wheat flour
- Olive oil spray

Instructions:

1. **Preheat Oven:** Preheat your oven to 375°F (190°C).
2. **Prepare the Chiles:** Carefully make a slit along the length of each chile to create an opening. Remove the seeds, being careful to keep the chiles intact.
3. **Mix the Filling:** In a mixing bowl, combine the cooked quinoa, corn, black beans, tomatoes, red onion, garlic, half of the cheese, cumin, and smoked paprika if using. Season with salt and pepper to taste.
4. **Stuff the Chiles:** Gently stuff each chile with the quinoa mixture, being careful not to overfill. Close the slit of each chile by pressing the edges together lightly.
5. **Coat the Chiles:** Dip each stuffed chile first in whole wheat flour, then in the beaten eggs.
6. **Bake:** Place the chiles on a baking sheet lined with parchment paper. Lightly spray the chiles with olive oil spray. Bake in the preheated oven for 25-30 minutes or until the chiles are golden and crispy.
7. **Add Cheese:** Sprinkle the remaining cheese over the chiles and bake for an additional 5 minutes, or until the cheese is melted and bubbly.
8. **Serve:** Remove from oven and let them rest for a few minutes before serving.

Nutritional Information (per serving):

- **Calories:** Approximately 220 kcal
- **Protein:** 12 g
- **Carbohydrates:** 28 g
- **Fat:** 8 g (Varies with cheese and olive oil used)
- **Fiber:** 5 g
- **Sodium:** Moderate (depends on cheese and seasoning)

Chef's Note:

- The quinoa provides a high-protein and fiber-rich alternative to traditional meat fillings.
- Using whole wheat flour and baking instead of frying makes this dish lower in calories and fat.
- You can adjust the level of heat by choosing milder or hotter New Mexico green chiles.

Steak and Shrimp Fajitas

- 4-6 servings

Enjoy your healthy and flavorful Surf and Turf Fajitas, a delightful twist on a classic New Mexican dish!

Ingredients:

- Lean Steak (such as flank or sirloin), 1 lb, thinly sliced
- Shrimp, peeled and deveined, 1 lb
- Red Onion, 1, thinly sliced
- Bell Peppers (red and yellow), 2, thinly sliced
- Garlic Cloves, 2, minced
- Lime Juice, from 2 limes
- Cilantro, ½ cup, chopped (optional)
- Olive Oil, 2 tbsp
- Whole Wheat or Low-Carb Tortillas, 8-10

Spices for Marinade:

- Cumin, 1 tsp
- Chili Powder, 1 tsp
- Paprika, 1 tsp
- Oregano, ½ tsp
- Salt and Pepper, to taste

Instructions:

1. Marinate the Protein:
   1. In a bowl, combine lime juice, olive oil, cumin, chili powder, paprika, oregano, salt, and pepper. Divide the marinade between the shrimp and steak in separate bowls. Toss to coat evenly and let them marinate for at least 30 minutes, preferably in the fridge.
2. Prepare Vegetables:
   1. While the protein is marinating, slice the onions and bell peppers. Mince the garlic and set aside.
3. Cook Steak:
   1. Heat a large skillet or grill pan over medium-high heat. Add a tablespoon of olive oil. Place the marinated steak slices in the pan and cook for about 2-3 minutes on each side, or until they reach your desired level of doneness. Remove from the pan and keep warm.
4. Cook Shrimp:
   1. In the same pan, add the shrimp. Cook for about 2 minutes on each side or until they turn pink and opaque. Remove from the pan and keep warm.
5. Sauté Vegetables:
   1. In the same pan, add a bit more oil if needed and sauté the onions and bell peppers until they are soft and slightly charred. Add the minced garlic in the last minute of cooking.
6. Assemble Fajitas:
   1. Warm the tortillas on the skillet or in the microwave. On each tortilla, lay down a base of the sautéed vegetables, then add slices of steak and a few shrimp. Garnish with fresh cilantro if desired.
7. Serve:

1. Serve the fajitas with sides of guacamole, salsa, and sour cream if desired. You can also offer lime wedges for an extra zing.

Nutritional Information (per serving):

- **Calories:** Approx. 350-400
- **Carbs:** Approx. 20-25g
- **Protein:** Approx. 35-40g
- **Fat: Approx.** 15-20g
- **Sodium:** Moderate

Vegetarian Tamales

- 12 tamales

These vegetarian tamales are a healthy and delicious twist on a traditional New Mexican dish. Enjoy the blend of fresh vegetables, quinoa, and aromatic spices wrapped in a soft masa dough!

Ingredients

For the Dough:

- 2 cups masa harina
- 1/2 cup extra virgin olive oil or avocado oil
- 1 teaspoon baking powder
- 1/2 teaspoon salt
- 1 1/2 cups vegetable broth or water

For the Filling:

- 1 tablespoon olive oil
- 1 small onion, finely chopped
- 2 cloves garlic, minced
- 1 cup diced zucchini
- 1 cup diced yellow squash
- 1/2 cup corn kernels (fresh or frozen)
- 1 cup cooked quinoa

- 1 teaspoon ground cumin
- 1/2 teaspoon smoked paprika
- Salt and pepper, to taste
- 1/2 cup shredded low-fat cheese (optional)

Additional:

- Corn husks, soaked in warm water for at least 30 minutes

Instructions

1. Prepare the Corn Husks:
    - Soak the corn husks in warm water for 30 minutes to make them pliable.
2. Make the Dough:
    - In a large bowl, mix together the masa harina, oil, baking powder, and salt.
    - Gradually add the vegetable broth, mixing until the dough is soft and pliable. If it's too dry, add more broth.
    - Let the dough rest for 30 minutes.
3. Cook the Filling:
    - Heat olive oil in a skillet over medium heat. Add onion and garlic, and sauté until soft.
    - Add zucchini, yellow squash, and corn. Cook until the vegetables are tender.
    - Stir in the cooked quinoa, cumin, smoked paprika, and season with salt and pepper.
    - Cook for another 5 minutes, then set aside to cool.
4. Assemble the Tamales:
    - Drain the corn husks and pat dry.
    - Take a husk, and spread about 2 tablespoons of dough in the center.

- Add a spoonful of the vegetable-quinoa filling and a sprinkle of cheese (if using).
- Fold the sides of the husk in, then fold the bottom up. Tie with a strip of corn husk or string.

5. Steam the Tamales:
    - Fill a large pot with a few inches of water and place a steamer basket inside.
    - Arrange the tamales standing up in the basket.
    - Cover and steam for about 60 minutes, or until the dough is firm and pulls away from the husk.

6. Serve:
    - Let the tamales cool for a few minutes before serving.
    - They can be enjoyed with salsa, guacamole, or your favorite sauce.

Nutritional Information (per tamale):

- Calories: 180 kcal
- Protein: 4 g
- Fat: 8 g
- Carbohydrates: 24 g
- Fiber: 3 g
- Sugar: 1 g
- Sodium: 200 mg

Chapter 8

Desserts

Rice Pudding

- 6 servings

This healthy version of rice pudding maintains the creamy texture and comforting flavors of the traditional dessert, but with a healthier twist. The use of brown rice and almond milk not only reduces the calorie content but also enhances the dish with a nutty flavor and added nutrients. The orange zest and cinnamon bring a warm, fragrant aroma that complements the natural sweetness of honey or agave syrup. Enjoy this delightful and nutritious dessert from the Healthy New Mexican Kitchen!

Ingredients:

- 1 cup brown rice (uncooked)
- 4 cups almond milk, unsweetened
- 1/4 cup honey or agave syrup (for a natural sweetener)
- 1 cinnamon stick
- Zest of 1 orange
- 1/2 tsp vanilla extract
- 1/4 tsp salt
- 1/4 cup raisins (optional)
- 1/4 cup chopped almonds (for garnish)
- Ground cinnamon for dusting

Instructions:

1. **Cook Rice:** In a medium saucepan, cook the brown rice as per package instructions. Brown rice is chosen for its higher fiber content compared to white rice.
2. **Combine Ingredients:** In the same saucepan over medium heat, add the almond milk, honey or agave syrup, cinnamon stick, orange zest, and salt to the cooked rice. Stir well to combine.
3. **Simmer:** Bring the mixture to a gentle simmer, stirring occasionally. Be careful to keep the heat low to avoid burning the milk.
4. **Thicken Pudding:** Continue to cook for about 25-30 minutes, or until the mixture thickens to your desired consistency. The rice will absorb the almond milk, thickening the pudding naturally without the need for cream or eggs.
5. **Add Raisins:** If using, add the raisins about halfway through the simmering process. They will plump up and add natural sweetness to the pudding.
6. **Finish & Serve:** Once thickened, remove from heat and discard the cinnamon stick. Stir in the vanilla extract. Serve the rice pudding either warm or chilled.
7. **Garnish:** Garnish with chopped almonds and a dusting of ground cinnamon before serving.

Nutritional Information (per serving):

- Calories: Approx. 200
- Carbohydrates: Approx. 3 g
- Fiber: Approx. 3g
- Protein: Approx. 4g
- Fat: Approx. 4g

Almond Flour Biscochitos

- 1 cookie per serving

Biscochitos, the state cookie of New Mexico, are traditionally enjoyed during festive occasions. This healthier version uses almond flour, reducing carbs and adding a nutritious twist to this beloved treat.

Ingredients:

- 2 cups almond flour
- 1/2 cup unsalted butter, softened
- 1/2 cup granulated erythritol or another sugar substitute
- 1 large egg
- 1 tsp vanilla extract
- 1 tsp anise extract
- 1/2 tsp baking powder
- 1/4 tsp salt
- 1/4 cup cinnamon sugar (made with sugar substitute and cinnamon)

Instructions:

1. **Preheat Oven and Prepare Baking Sheet:**

- Preheat your oven to 350°F (175°C). Line a baking sheet with parchment paper.

2. **Cream Butter and Sugar:**
   - In a large mixing bowl, beat the softened butter with the erythritol until creamy and well combined.

3. **Add Egg and Extracts:**
   - Mix in the egg, vanilla extract, and anise extract, beating until fully integrated.

4. **Combine Dry Ingredients:**
   - In a separate bowl, whisk together the almond flour, baking powder, and salt.

5. **Mix Dry Ingredients with Wet:**
   - Gradually add the dry ingredients to the wet mixture, stirring until a dough forms.

6. **Form Cookies:**
   - Roll the dough into small balls, about 1 inch in diameter. Place them on the prepared baking sheet.

7. **Flatten and Sprinkle:**
   - Gently flatten each ball with the bottom of a glass. Sprinkle the tops with cinnamon sugar.

8. **Bake:**
   - Bake in the preheated oven for 12-15 minutes, or until the edges are lightly golden.

9. **Cool:**
   - Allow the biscochitos to cool on the baking sheet for 5 minutes before transferring them to a wire rack to cool completely.

10. **Serve and Enjoy:**
    - Serve your almond flour biscochitos with a cup of yerba buena tea or your favorite coffee.

Nutritional Information (per cookie):

- Calories: 90

- Carbohydrates: 2g
- Protein: 2g
- Fat: 8g
- Sodium: 25mg
- Sugar: 0.5g

Green Chile Apple Pie

- 8 servings

Incorporate the unique flavors of New Mexico into a classic dessert with this Green Chile Apple Pie. This recipe combines the sweetness of apples with the subtle heat of green chiles, creating a delightful and unexpected fusion of flavors.

Ingredients

Pie Crust:

- 2 1/2 cups whole wheat flour
- 1 tsp salt
- 1 cup unsalted butter, chilled and cubed
- 1/2 cup ice water

Filling:

- 4 large apples, peeled, cored, and thinly sliced
- 1/2 cup brown sugar or a sugar substitute
- 1/2 cup chopped roasted green chiles (mild or medium)
- 2 tbsp whole wheat flour
- 2 tsp ground cinnamon
- 1/2 tsp nutmeg

- Juice of 1 lemon

Egg Wash:

- 1 egg, beaten
- 1 tbsp water

Instructions:

1. **Prepare the Pie Crust:**
    - In a large bowl, mix together 2 1/2 cups whole wheat flour and 1 tsp salt. Add the chilled, cubed butter, using your fingers or a pastry cutter to blend until the mixture resembles coarse crumbs.
    - Gradually add ice water, stirring until the dough comes together. Divide the dough in half, form into disks, wrap in plastic, and refrigerate for at least 1 hour.
2. **Make the Filling:**
    - In a large bowl, combine sliced apples, brown sugar, green chiles, 2 tbsp flour, cinnamon, nutmeg, and lemon juice. Toss to coat the apples evenly.
3. **Assemble the Pie:**
    - Preheat your oven to 375°F (190°C).
    - On a floured surface, roll out one disk of dough to fit a 9-inch pie pan. Place the crust in the pan, trimming any excess.
    - Pour the apple-green chile filling into the crust.
    - Roll out the second dough disk and place it over the filling. Trim, seal, and flute the edges.
    - Cut slits in the top crust to allow steam to escape. Brush the crust with the beaten egg mixed with 1 tbsp water.
4. **Bake:**

- Bake in the preheated oven for about 50 minutes or until the crust is golden brown and the filling is bubbly.
- If the edges brown too quickly, cover them with foil.

5. Cool and Serve:
    - Allow the pie to cool before serving. This helps the filling set and makes slicing easier.
    - Serve with a scoop of low-fat vanilla ice cream or a dollop of whipped cream, if desired.

Nutritional Information (per serving):

- Servings: 8
- Calories: 350 kcal
- Carbohydrates: 45 g
- Protein: 5 g
- Fat: 18 g
- Saturated Fat: 11 g
- Cholesterol: 60 mg
- Sodium: 300 mg
- Fiber: 5 g
- Sugar: 20 g (varies with sugar substitute)

Red Chile Brownies

- 12 servings

Enjoy your Healthy New Mexican Kitchen Red Chile Brownies, a deliciously unique dessert that combines traditional New Mexican flavors with a health-conscious approach!

Ingredients:

- 1 cup almond flour
- 1/2 cup unsweetened cocoa powder
- 1/4 cup finely ground red chile powder (mild or medium heat, as per preference)
- 1 teaspoon baking powder
- 1/2 teaspoon salt
- 3 large eggs, at room temperature
- 1/2 cup coconut oil, melted and cooled
- 1 cup erythritol or another sugar substitute
- 1 teaspoon vanilla extract
- Optional: 1/2 cup chopped walnuts or pecans

Instructions:

1. **Preheat Oven and Prepare Pan:**
    - Preheat your oven to 350°F (175°C).
    - Grease an 8-inch square baking pan and line it with parchment paper for easy removal of the brownies.

2. Mix Dry Ingredients:
   - In a medium bowl, whisk together the almond flour, cocoa powder, red chile powder, baking powder, and salt.
3. Combine Wet Ingredients:
   - In a separate large bowl, whisk the eggs.
   - Add the melted coconut oil, erythritol (or sugar substitute), and vanilla extract, whisking until well combined.
4. Combine Wet and Dry Ingredients:
   - Gradually add the dry ingredients to the wet mixture, stirring until just combined.
   - If using, fold in the chopped walnuts or pecans.
5. Bake the Brownies:
   - Pour the batter into the prepared baking pan, smoothing the top with a spatula.
   - Bake for 25-30 minutes, or until a toothpick inserted in the center comes out mostly clean with a few moist crumbs.
6. Cool and Serve:
   - Allow the brownies to cool in the pan for about 10 minutes, then lift them out using the parchment paper and transfer to a wire rack to cool completely.
   - Cut into squares and serve.

Nutritional Information (Per Serving):

- Calories: Approx. 150-180 (varies with substitutions)
- Net Carbs: Approx. 3-5g (varies with substitutions)
- Protein: 4g
- Fat: 12-15g

Chef's Note:

- The red chile powder adds a unique New Mexican twist to these brownies, providing a subtle warmth that complements the rich chocolate flavor.
- Erythritol, a sugar alcohol, is used as a healthier alternative to sugar. It has a negligible impact on blood sugar and calorie count.
- Almond flour is a gluten-free and low-carb alternative to traditional flour, making these brownies suitable for those on a gluten-free or keto diet.

Natillas (New Mexico Custard)

- 6 servings

Natillas is a traditional New Mexican dessert, a creamy custard that's a lighter alternative to many heavy desserts. This version of Natillas is modified to fit a healthier diet, reducing sugar and using low-fat milk.

Ingredients:

- 4 cups low-fat milk
- 3 large eggs
- 2 tablespoons cornstarch
- 1/3 cup honey (or a sweetener of your choice, adjusted to taste)
- 1 cinnamon stick
- 1 teaspoon pure vanilla extract
- Ground cinnamon, for garnish

Instructions:

1. **Heat the Milk:** In a large saucepan, gently heat the milk and cinnamon stick over medium heat. Bring to a simmer, then remove from heat. Do not boil.

2. **Mix Eggs and Cornstarch:** In a bowl, whisk together the eggs, cornstarch, and honey until smooth. This mixture will thicken the custard.
3. **Temper the Egg Mixture:** Gradually whisk about a cup of the hot milk into the egg mixture to temper it. This prevents the eggs from scrambling.
4. **Combine and Cook:** Pour the egg mixture back into the saucepan with the remaining milk. Cook over low heat, stirring constantly, until the mixture thickly coats the back of a spoon, about 10-15 minutes.
5. **Add Vanilla:** Remove from heat. Discard the cinnamon stick and stir in the vanilla extract.
6. **Cool and Serve:** Pour the natillas into serving dishes. Let them cool to room temperature, then chill in the refrigerator. Garnish with a sprinkle of ground cinnamon before serving.

Nutritional Information (per serving):

- **Calories:** 180
- **Carbohydrates:** 24g
- **Protein:** 9g
- **Fat:** 5g
- **Cholesterol:** 95mg
- **Sodium:** 110mg
- **Sugar:** 20g (Natural sugars from honey and milk)

Chef's Note:

- For a vegan version, use almond or coconut milk and a plant-based egg substitute.
- Adjust the sweetness to your preference. Honey can be replaced with maple syrup, agave nectar, or a sugar substitute.

Chapter 9

Drinks

Blue Corn Atole

- 4 servings

Blue Corn Atole (Atole de Maíz Azul) is a warm, comforting drink rooted in New Mexican and Native American traditions. This healthier twist on the classic atole uses blue cornmeal, known for its nutty flavor and higher protein content, making it a nutritious and satisfying beverage.

Ingredients:

- 1/2 cup blue cornmeal
- 4 cups water
- 1 cinnamon stick
- 1/4 cup honey or agave syrup (adjust to taste)
- 1/2 teaspoon pure vanilla extract
- Pinch of salt

Instructions:

1. **Combine Water and Cornmeal:** In a large saucepan, gradually whisk the blue cornmeal into the water, ensuring there are no lumps.
2. **Add Cinnamon:** Add the cinnamon stick to the mixture.
3. **Cook the Atole:** Place the saucepan over medium heat. Stir constantly until the mixture starts to thicken (about

10-15 minutes). The consistency should be similar to a thin porridge.
4. **Flavor the Atole:** Once thickened, remove the cinnamon stick. Stir in the honey or agave syrup, vanilla extract, and a pinch of salt. Mix well.
5. **Simmer:** Reduce the heat and let the atole simmer for another 5 minutes, stirring occasionally.
6. **Serve:** Remove from heat. Pour the atole into mugs and serve warm.

Nutritional Information (per serving):

- **Calories:** 120
- **Protein:** 2g
- **Carbohydrates:** 27g
- **Fat:** 1g
- **Sodium:** 50mg
- **Fiber:** 2g

Chef's Note:

- For a creamier atole, you can substitute one cup of water with almond milk or another plant-based milk.
- Blue cornmeal can be found in specialty food stores or online.
- Adjust the sweetness according to your preference.
- The drink can be garnished with a sprinkle of ground cinnamon or a cinnamon stick for presentation.

Spicy Champurrado

- 4 servings

Champurrado is a traditional Mexican chocolate drink thickened with masa and infused with warm spices. This version adds a spicy twist, perfect for those who love a little heat with their sweet.

Ingredients:

- 4 cups of water
- 2 cinnamon sticks
- 1 star anise
- 1/4 cup masa harina (corn flour)
- 2 cups of unsweetened almond milk
- 100g dark chocolate, chopped (preferably 70% cocoa)
- 1/4 cup raw honey or agave syrup
- 1 teaspoon vanilla extract
- 1/2 teaspoon chili powder (adjust to taste)
- A pinch of cayenne pepper (optional for extra heat)
- Ground cinnamon, for garnish

Instructions:

1. **Spice Infusion:** In a large pot, bring the water to a boil with the cinnamon sticks and star anise. Reduce to a simmer and let it steep for about 10 minutes to infuse the water with the spices.
2. **Masa Preparation:** In a separate bowl, whisk the masa harina with a half cup of the infused water to create a smooth, lump-free mixture.
3. **Chocolate Mixture:** Add the almond milk, chocolate, honey, and vanilla extract to the pot with the infused water. Warm over medium heat, stirring constantly until the chocolate is fully melted.
4. **Thicken the Champurrado:** Gradually pour the masa mixture into the pot, whisking continuously to prevent lumps. Continue to cook over medium heat, stirring often, until the mixture thickens to a creamy consistency (about 10-15 minutes).
5. **Add Spice:** Stir in the chili powder and cayenne pepper. Adjust the seasoning to taste.
6. **Serve:** Remove from heat. Discard the cinnamon sticks and star anise. Serve the champurrado in mugs, garnished with a sprinkle of ground cinnamon.

Nutritional Information (Per Serving)

- Calories: Approx. 200-250 kcal
- Carbohydrates: 30g
- Protein: 3g
- Fat: 10g
- Sugar: 15g (depending on sweetener used)

Chef's Note:

- For a less spicy version, reduce the amount of chili powder and omit the cayenne pepper.

- You can substitute almond milk with another plant-based milk for a different flavor profile.
- The thickness of the champurrado can be adjusted by varying the amount of masa harina.

Horchata

- 8 servings

This version of Horchata is a lighter, healthier take on the traditional Mexican drink, perfect for those who enjoy the sweet and spicy flavors of this classic beverage while maintaining a health-conscious diet. Enjoy this refreshing drink as a unique addition to your meal or a delightful treat on its own!

Ingredients:

- 1 cup uncooked long grain white rice
- 4 cups water
- 2 cinnamon sticks
- 1/3 cup sweetener (like honey, agave syrup, or a sugar substitute for a lower-calorie option)
- 2 tsp vanilla extract
- 4 cups unsweetened almond milk (or any preferred non-dairy milk)
- Ground cinnamon, for garnish
- Ice cubes

Instructions:

1. Rice and Cinnamon Infusion:
    1. Rinse the rice under cold water until the water runs clear.

2. In a large bowl, combine the rinsed rice, cinnamon sticks, and 4 cups of water. Cover and let it soak overnight at room temperature.

2. **Blending:**
   1. Remove the cinnamon sticks from the soaked rice mixture.
   2. Transfer the rice and water to a blender. Blend until the rice is completely ground.
3. **Straining:**
   1. Place a fine mesh strainer over a large bowl. Pour the blended rice mixture through it to remove the rice solids. Discard solids.
4. **Adding Flavor:**
   1. To the strained liquid, add the sweetener, vanilla extract, and almond milk. Stir well until all the ingredients are fully combined.
5. **Chilling:**
   1. Refrigerate the horchata until it's completely chilled. This usually takes about 1-2 hours.
6. **Serving:**
   1. Serve the horchata over ice, garnished with a sprinkle of ground cinnamon on top.
7. **Optional Adjustments:**
   1. For a creamier texture, consider adding a little light coconut milk.
   2. Adjust the sweetness according to taste. You can also add a touch of nutmeg for extra flavor.

Nutritional Information (per serving, 1 cup):

- **Calories:** Approximately 90-110 kcal (varies based on sweetener and milk used)
- **Carbs:** 18g
- **Fat:** 1g

- **Protein:** 1g
- **Sugar:** Varies on sweetener used

Yerba Buena with Lemon

- This recipe serves 1. Multiply the ingredients proportionally for more servings.

Yerba Buena, commonly known as spearmint, has long been cherished in traditional New Mexican herbal medicine for its refreshing aroma and soothing properties. Combined with the zest of lemon, this tea offers a delightful and healthful beverage, perfect for relaxation or aiding digestion.

Ingredients:

- 1 tablespoon fresh Yerba Buena leaves (spearmint) or 1 teaspoon dried Yerba Buena
- 1 cup boiling water
- 1-2 teaspoons of honey (optional, for sweetness)
- Fresh lemon slices or 2 teaspoons of fresh lemon juice
- Lemon zest (optional, for garnish)

Instructions:

1. **Prepare the Yerba Buena:** If using fresh Yerba Buena leaves, gently rinse them under cold water. If you're using dried leaves, measure out the required amount.

2. **Steep the Tea:** Place the Yerba Buena leaves in a cup or a tea infuser. Pour one cup of boiling water over the leaves. Let them steep for about 5-7 minutes. The longer you steep, the stronger the flavor will be.
3. **Add Lemon and Sweeten:** After steeping, remove the leaves. Add fresh lemon slices or lemon juice to the tea. If you prefer a sweeter taste, stir in honey to your liking.
4. **Garnish and Serve:** Garnish with a sprinkle of lemon zest for an extra burst of flavor and aroma. Serve the tea hot for a comforting experience or chill for a refreshing iced tea option.

Nutritional Information (per serving)

- **Calories:** 4 (without honey)
- **Carbohydrates:** 1g
- **Sugars:** 0g (without honey)

Health Benefits:

Yerba Buena is known for its digestive and calming properties, making this tea an excellent choice for soothing the stomach. Lemon adds a dose of vitamin C and aids in digestion, while honey provides a natural sweetening option without the need for refined sugars.

Chef's Note:

Yerba Buena tea with lemon is versatile. Feel free to adjust the amount of lemon and honey to suit your taste preferences. This tea is perfect as a morning refreshment, a digestive aid after meals, or a calming evening drink.

Chapter 10

Healthy Cooking Techniques and Tips

Choosing The Right Ingredients for Healthier Cooking

Embracing a healthy New Mexican kitchen starts with selecting the right ingredients. This chapter focuses on how to choose ingredients that are not only nutritious but also uphold the authentic flavors of New Mexican cuisine.

Fresh Produce

- Vegetables: Opt for a variety of colorful vegetables like bell peppers, tomatoes, onions, garlic, and leafy greens. These are packed with vitamins and minerals.
- Fruits: Incorporate fruits like apples, berries, and citrus fruits for natural sweetness and a vitamin boost.

Lean Proteins

- Poultry: Choose skinless chicken or turkey as healthier alternatives to red meat.
- Fish: Trout and other lean fish are excellent for grilling or baking.

- Legumes: Beans, especially pinto and black beans, are great protein sources and are staple in New Mexican cuisine.

Whole Grains

- Corn: Use whole corn kernels or stone-ground cornmeal for authentic flavor and added fiber.
- Whole Wheat: Opt for whole wheat flour or other whole grain flours for baking.

Healthy Fats

- Avocado: Rich in healthy fats and perfect for guacamole or salads.
- Nuts and Seeds: Add crunch and nutrients to dishes with almonds, pecans, or pumpkin seeds.
- Olive Oil: A healthier alternative to butter or lard for cooking.

Herbs and Spices

- Chiles: Hatch green and red chiles are the essence of New Mexican cuisine, adding flavor without calories.
- Cilantro: A traditional herb used for its fresh, citrusy flavor.
- Cumin, Oregano, and Garlic: These spices add depth to dishes without extra fat or salt.

Techniques to Enhance Flavor without Extra Calories

Creating flavorful dishes without adding extra calories is an art. This chapter explores cooking techniques that enhance the natural flavors of ingredients while keeping dishes healthy.

Roasting and Grilling

- **Vegetables and Meats:** Roasting or grilling brings out natural sweetness and smokiness, reducing the need for added fats and sugars.

Steaming

- **Preserves Nutrients:** Steaming vegetables and fish preserves their nutrients and natural flavors.

Sautéing and Stir-Frying

- **Use Broth or Water:** Instead of oil, use a small amount of broth or water for sautéing vegetables and meats.

Slow Cooking

- **Develops Flavors:** Slow cooking stews and soups melds flavors together without needing excess fat or salt.

Herbs and Spices

- **Natural Flavor Enhancers:** Use a variety of herbs and spices to add complexity to dishes without relying on fat and salt.

Acidic Ingredients

- **Brighten Flavors:** Adding a splash of lime or vinegar can brighten up a dish, enhancing its overall flavor profile.

Incorporating these ingredients and techniques into your cooking routine will help you create healthier New Mexican dishes that don't compromise on taste. Enjoy experimenting with these healthy twists on traditional recipes!

Hello, I'm Chef's Palette, born and raised under the expansive skies of northern New Mexico. My journey with food began in the kitchens of my childhood, where the rich, traditional flavors of New Mexican cuisine were a daily celebration. These early experiences ignited my passion for cooking and inspired me to explore the culinary arts more deeply.

Growing up, I was surrounded by a tapestry of tastes and aromas that shaped my understanding of food. From the hearty stews and spicy chilies of my hometown to the sweet scent of piñon wood burning in the hearth, every meal was a testament to our rich cultural heritage. This foundation has been the cornerstone of my approach to cooking – creating recipes that honor the traditional foods I grew up with while infusing them with a modern, health-conscious twist.

My culinary journey took a new turn as I began exploring other cuisines. This exploration broadened my palate and deepened my appreciation for the diversity of flavors and techniques from around the world. It's been a thrilling adventure to meld these international influences with the robust flavors of New Mexican cuisine.

In an effort to share my passion and expertise, I started working on Fiverr, offering my services to help people create customizable recipes that cater to their unique lifestyles. Whether it's adapting a classic dish to fit dietary needs or crafting a completely new recipe, my goal is to bring joy and health through food.

For personalized recipe creation that harmonizes your dietary preferences with the rich flavors of New Mexican cuisine and beyond, visit my Fiverr page at fiverr.com/ezhomechef. I look forward to crafting a culinary experience that's tailored just for you!

fiverr.com/
ezhomechef

www.ingramcontent.com/pod-product-compliance
Lightning Source LLC
LaVergne TN
LVHW021951060526
838201LV00049B/1671